A Daughter's Cry and a Father's Response

Inspirational Devotions

ANNAIKA DASTINE

ISBN 979-8-89345-405-5 (paperback)
ISBN 979-8-89345-406-2 (digital)

Christian Faith Publishing
832 Park Avenue
Meadville, PA 16335
www.christianfaithpublishing.com

Printed in the United States of America

Jesus spoke, "I am the light of the world.
If you follow me, you won't have to walk in darkness,
because you will have the light that leads to life."

—John 8:12 NLT

INTRODUCTION

HELLO, MY FRIEND! Thank you for joining me in this life journey with Jesus. Before you read these devotionals, I would like to share with you that I fought with God for many years to not write this book. My husband is God's witness to this. In May 2019, I cried and prayed to God, asking, "What is my purpose as His servant and daughter?"

As I was having this intimate connection with my Father, Lord, and Savior, I heard Him clearly whisper to me, "You were not rescued by Me for your own satisfaction but to reach out to My children who are seeking an intimate relationship with Me. I am calling you to be My voice! Your struggles with your physical pain are obstacles from the enemy to deter you from your true purpose, but I will use it for My glory. Trust Me!" At that moment, I recalled Job's words,

> My ears had heard of you but now my eyes have
> seen you. (Job 42:5 NIV)

I decided to repent and said just as Mary said to the Angel of God in Luke 1:38, "I am the Lord's servant."

I will obey even though I am unworthy of this call, and it does not make any sense. Why me? I have no idea what I am doing or what I should do with this call. All I know is I am choosing to be obedient.

I share this to tell everyone who opens this book that God does not make mistakes, and everything happens as a part of His perfect, divine plan for you and me! My prayer is that God will use me as a vessel to minister and inspire everyone He allows to read this book to draw closer to His throne, no matter where you are in your walk with Jesus. Or maybe you don't even believe in or know Jesus. I humbly pray that Jesus manifests His will to you through my life experiences and Bible studies and that God—through the Holy Spirit—has inspired me to share these devotionals and reflections with you. Let it be known, I am not a Bible scholar or a Bible guru. I am simply a sinner who has been touched by a Healer. I simply want to share about His everlasting grace, compassion, and warnings that I have learned reading the Bible. My earnest prayer to God about this ministry is to teach me through this journey how to walk and be led by His Spirit. I do not want to gratify the sinful nature in me by using the freedom He gives through the Holy Spirit for my own selfish purpose (Galatians 5:13). I pray that as I once read by a writer who was given great advice by her father when she decided to publish a book, which resonates with me as I embark on my own journey, "I give you my weakness so that it may lead to your strength" (*Secure in Heart*, Robin Weidner 2006). I would like to say to you today, as I share my broken self and the power of God continuing to mend my life, I trust that it may lead you to your own journey of healing.

Spiritual Foundation

> This is what the Lord says: "When seventy years are completed for Babylon, I will come to you and fulfill my good promise to bring you back to this place. For I know the plans I have for you," declares the Lord, "plans to prosper you and not to harm you, plans to give you hope and a future. Then you will call on me and come and pray to me, and I will listen to you. You will seek me and find me when you seek me with all your heart. I will be found by you," declares the Lord, "and will bring you back from captivity. I will gather you from all the nations and places where I have banished you," declares the Lord, "and will bring

you back to the place from which I carried you
into exile." (Jeremiah 29:10–14 NIV)

Reading these scriptures for the first time as a young four-teen-year-old girl, they sounded so powerful and hopeful. Initially, I thought this promise only applied to the Jews during their time of struggle. However, as I processed these scriptures, I continued to see God's work in my life over the past thirty-four years and how He rescued me. I knew then, and I certainly know now, that God was calling me out of captivity to reconcile me back to my destiny: which is to have a relationship with Him. He was not calling me to join a church, religion, or social club. His call was simple: "Annaika, I want you back because you belong to Me." I genuinely believe this call is for you as well!

> Very rarely will anyone die for a righteous person, though for a good person someone might possibly dare to die. But God demonstrates his own love for us in this: While we were still sinners, Christ died for us. (Romans 5:6–8 NIV)

These scriptures are one of the major rocks in my foundation with Jesus! Knowing that He did not die for me because I was "good" but because I was broken, sick, and drowning in my mess. This is an incredible love language that is beyond my comprehension. That love language is extended to you as well, no matter where you are in life. This devotional book is one of many that will focus on Jesus's call for each of you, not as a chore or something that you are forced to do but as an individual decision to have a personal relationship with Him.

DEVOTIONALS

My First Personal Encounter with Jesus

I RECOGNIZE MY encounter and journey with Jesus may not be your typical conversion story. My word of encouragement is simple: Give Jesus, the Messiah, a chance, and I guarantee you, you will have your own rescue story. One of my favorite stories in the Bible is Jesus's encounter with the woman at the well. The response of the people from her town is my prayer for anyone who joins me in this journey with Jesus.

> Then the Samaritans said to the woman, "We no longer believe just because of what you told us, but now we've heard him ourselves and are convinced that he really is the true Savior of the world!" (John 4:42 TPT)

Who is this Jesus? A desperate little girl cried out to an unknown God that she heard about but had no concrete evidence or knowledge of His existence. That little girl was me!

> In my distress I called to the Lord; I cried to my God for help. From his temple he heard my

voice; my cry came before him, into his ears.
(Psalm 18:6 NIV)

I was born on the island of Haiti. From the time I recall my existence in this world, I was plagued with different sicknesses that robbed me of my childhood. I remember sitting and watching my cousins playing and wishing that I knew what it was like to feel well and enjoy the gift of playing. I grew up in a family that practices witchcraft known as voodoo, which is considered a religion in Haiti. I thought that was normal life, and it was fun. As a five-year-old girl, I learned some of the songs, dances, and a few of the prayers that they recite before starting their worship service to the underworld spirits. I witnessed things that seemed scary and unimaginable, things that the United States and the Hollywood world would consider fiction. The purpose of my writings is not to glorify Satan; it is to call my readers to the simple fact that Satan is real. Growing up, I saw how Satan manifests through fear, poverty, and false hope through the voodoo religion; however, in the United States, it is my opinion that he manifests through wealth, greed, materialism, fear, false security, and power.

My first encounter with Jesus is one I will never forget. Jesus showed up at the right time to rescue me while I was hopeless, confused, and scared. I felt empty as a nine-year-old girl. As a child, I was constantly sick, experiencing chronic weakness, high fevers, headaches, and fainting spells. During that time, a family member who lives in America came to Haiti and explained to me that my sickness was due to a broken promise that was made while my mother was pregnant. The promise was for me to become a priestess servant of an evil spirit. The family member stated that there was still hope for me to get well, but my father refused to give me the money. He expressed that "he would rather bury me with the money." The family member's story was corroborated by two other family members; as a result, I developed resentment against my father, whom I had never met. He left Haiti when I was just a toddler. But glory be to Jesus, my relationship with my father has been repaired, which I hope to share in more detail someday. During that period, my family was seeking treatment for me through medical doctors and voodoo priests.

Throughout this period of my suffering, I remember a woman by the name of Madame Raymond. She would often tell me, "I am praying for you because only Jesus can deliver you." As a child, I had no idea what that meant and just smiled at her. As time went by, I noticed she would have gatherings at her house where her church would come, singing while playing instruments. The interesting detail that I recall is that some of the instruments they used were also utilized during the voodoo service, like tambourines. However, they were singing with great joy and praying as if they were talking to God; it felt different as I stood in their presence. There was a sense of calmness; no vile language or inappropriate behavior was part of their worship, as compared to the voodoo service celebration that my family had. I forgot to mention that I snuck out of my house a few times to go to Madame Raymond's house without my grandmother's or the people in my house's knowledge. I honestly do not know if they would have let me go there because I had witnessed my family and others in the community making fun of Madame Raymond, calling her crazy. Therefore, at an early age, I knew it was better not to ask. There was something pulling me to join them each time she hosted devotionals at her place. Now I know that something was the presence of the Holy Spirit of God. I can recall her smile as she welcomed me and asked the members of her church to pray over me for healing because I was always hospitalized, and they did. Little did I know, God was preparing my deliverance that year.

> For he has not despised my cries of deep despair.
> My first responder to my sufferings, and he didn't
> look the other way when I was in pain. He was
> there all the time, listening to the song of the
> afflicted. (Psalm 22:24 TPT)

Between the ages of eight and nine, I became very ill and missed most of my school days that year, which resulted in me being left behind a grade. At some point during the peak of my sickness, I became depressed, suicidal, and felt lonely. I can recall sitting at the front step of the house after a family member physically abused me, crying and wanting to die because I felt like an orphan. I did not know my parents because they both left for America when I was young.

During that year, I had another major episode of illness, and my family decided to try a home hospital. It was at that time my journey and purpose in this life changed forever. One morning, I woke up feeling sick and desperate. I made a simple prayer to Jesus, asking Him to help me. If what Madame Raymond had been saying about Him was true, I vowed to serve Him for the rest of my life if He helped me. As time went by, one afternoon while I was lying down on a bed under the place where they normally have voodoo service, I fainted, or so they thought. At that time, I went into a deep sleep and saw the roof of the space where I was lying down open and a voice like thunder said, "I have heard your cry," and a big hand came from the sky and gave me a Bible, saying, "In due time you will understand what this means."

Reflecting on my experience, Psalm 34:6 resonates with me; I was a poor, helpless, and harassed little girl who cried to the Lord, and He heard me. When I woke up from the vision, I remember seeing people around my bed attending to me, but it felt like I was far away. I rested for most of the afternoon. When I woke up, I was anxious to tell someone about my vision, but each time I attempted to tell different family members, I was not able to speak. The next day, I was lying on the bed in my grandmother's room when a family friend who was a voodoo servant came to visit me, and suddenly, I was able to speak. I remember telling him with excitement what had taken place the day before. Immediately, he began to curse the gods that he served and said, "You have been suffering since I knew you as a child. The God of heaven has chosen you to serve Him." He continued to testify, knowing that the God who called me was the true God, and encouraged me to follow His call. I honestly had no understanding of the content he was sharing because it was all new to me.

Although my journey with Jesus started that day, my walk with God has been a daily battle since. I am here to tell you, whatever you are going through, whatever your circumstance might be if Jesus can rescue me from hell as a little girl through a vision while evil spirits were tormenting me, He can do the same for you. Nothing is too big or too small for Jesus. When He says to you and me in Matthew 11:28, "Come to me, all you who are weary and burdened, and I will give you rest," He means it. I don't know what your hell might be. Could it be drug addiction, sexual abuse, domestic violence, sex addiction, rejection, depression, anxiety, your lifestyle, or you were once walking with the Lord and have lost your way? No matter what your burden might be, decide today that you will give Jesus a chance to give you the rest that you seek. Now if I tell you that your life will be trouble-free and all your problems will go away if you choose Jesus, that would be a lie. Jesus Himself says,

> In the world ye shall have tribulation: but be of good cheer; I have overcome the world. (John 16:33 KJV)

The most essential part of this passage is that our Lord Jesus has overcome the tribulation of this world so that you and I can receive reconciliation (Romans 5:11). You and I no longer have to live in the bondage of Satan's trap. You can be set free because Jesus promises,

> So if the son sets you free, you will be free indeed. (John 8:36 NIV)

If you are willing to take Him at His Word, I promise you that your life will change forever!

CHAPTER 2

The Battle for Our Soul

THE BATTLE FOR our soul began the day that God created humankind!

Eve: The First Daughter of the Living God
Genesis 2:4 and 3:1–24

How many of you, at various times in your life, have felt the feelings of shame and fear?

Shame, according to the *Webster's Dictionary*, is defined as "a painful emotion caused by a consciousness (or unconsciousness) of guilt, shortcomings, or impropriety."

Fear, according to the *Oxford Dictionary*, is defined as: "an unpleasant emotion caused by the belief that someone or something is dangerous, likely to cause pain, or a threat."

Have any of you ever struggled with feelings of guilt, regret, remorse, self-reproach, humiliation, disgrace, dishonor, failure, unworthiness, worthlessness, confusion, emptiness, hopelessness, and so on? You can fill in the blank. Feelings are part of who we are and are necessary for our survival. However, our feelings are usually triggered by positive or negative experiences, which dictate our behavior. The manifestation of our behavior from our feelings depends on the perception of the event that happens in our lives, which triggers our reaction. The way we interpret the events of our lives dictates how they impact our emotional and physical well-being.

What if I tell you these feelings are often connected to *shame* with the goal of destroying you physically, psychologically, and spiritually? What if I tell you there is a higher power who can free you from the shameful feelings that Satan enslaves you with? These shameful feelings, whether caused by our self-inflicted decisions or inflicted on us by others, often lead to depression, anxiety, isolation, self-devaluation, hopelessness, hatred, confusion, and, sadly, too often, the end of some lives by suicide. Many times, we choose to self-medicate with destructive behaviors such as drugs, alcohol, overachieving, underachieving, material things, revenge, unhealthy romantic relationships, and so on, all hoping to weaken the pain that is so unbearable. Shameful feelings have been ingrained so well in our lives that we do not even see them, especially if we strive to compensate for them with "success" or "life accomplishments."

If you ever feel the deep, empty void in your inner soul despite all your accomplishments in life, it is usually a clear indication that Satan has planted shame in your life. Or if you feel like you are never good enough, Satan has planted shame in your life. I am here to share with you how Jesus helped set me free from Satan's trap (Luke 4:18–19). I could share with you many examples of how Jesus has rescued me, but for this devotional, I will draw from one of the many traumatic events that took place in my life that He freed me from.

I remember the morning when I woke up from a nightmare that was hidden in the unconscious part of my brain for many years; this all started when I was nineteen years old. At the time, a midwife I was seeing for my routine yearly exam had observed my reaction when she attempted to complete my exam. After learning that I had always selected to complete a sonogram every year because I didn't want anyone touching me, she listened and empathized with me, and with a soft, gentle voice said, "From my experience, when a person has such a strong reaction to a GYN exam, it is because they have been a victim of sexual abuse." She followed her statement with a direct question: "Have you been a victim of sexual abuse? Has anyone ever touched you without your permission?" I looked at her with a perplexed look and decisively said no. I left that office troubled that morning. I kept thinking, why do I react in such a way as she mentioned during exams?

I remember deciding to fast and pray, asking God to reveal if there is a reason I am guarded and resent being touched by anyone. You know the saying "Be careful what you pray for!" After a week of prayer, one Sunday during a time of meditation at night, I started having memories that I had suppressed when I was seven years old flooding my mind. I felt weak, dirty, angry, ashamed, and guilty. I started blaming myself. I recall being told by the person I was her special friend as she repeatedly took advantage of me. The person also had me engage in shameful acts. I remember weeping as I called a close friend who came over the next morning before her job interview to pray and cry with me. I started blaming myself, asking, "Why did I not say anything to anyone?"

Reflecting on that period as a mental health worker, I was always sickly and did not get any positive attention besides being a sick child who was helpless. Looking back, being told by someone that I was special and that nobody should ever learn about our secret felt special at an early age. Facing those memories at the age of nineteen resulted in bitterness toward my parents and family members and Jesus, who I felt should have protected me. In my walk with Jesus, I began to wonder why God wanted me back because I felt broken. I started questioning, why did God allow this to happen? I started questioning my sexuality as well because my abuser was a female.

Facing what seemed like a monster in my life at the time was a true test of my faith in Jesus. I started asking several questions that we sometimes ask when our world seems to be turning upside down. I was in a spiritual battle where Satan was waging war for my soul, which led me to question God's love and sovereignty. I ponder on this question quite often: How could a loving God allow this horrible thing to happen to me? Psalm 139, which is now one of my favorite chapters, was not always so. In my anger toward God, I was no longer able to believe verse 14 of that Psalm:

> I praise you because I am fearfully and wonder-
> fully made.

During my inner battle with God, I felt like God wrongfully made me. Looking back, I thank God that despite all the bitterness toward Him, He did not give up on me. Instead, He allowed the Spirit of Truth, Counselor, Advocate, and Intercessor (John 14:25–26, 15:26, and 16:7) to open my eyes through the healing process to know Him deeper. Before I was able to heal spiritually, I had to heal in the physical form.

My next statement has nothing to do with the fact that I am a mental health professional but has everything to do with the fact that I am a testament that sitting with another person who is objective and being able to talk and process my thoughts and feelings works. There is power in validation and sorting through the hurt that has been inflicted on you or caused by your own mistakes. Yes, I went for therapy to work through many hurtful and painful things that have been part of my journey. It felt good to let the hurt, anger, and hopeless feelings out. However, I also learned therapy works for a while, and without a long-term plan, my healing process would be short-lived. Seeking counseling allowed me the clarity of mind to receive and listen to the voice of the Holy Spirit that was given to me on the day of baptism. The best analogy I can share to describe how seeking therapy helped me is that it allowed me to reject the flesh and my sinful nature desires (Galatians 5:16–21) so that I can be in fellowship with the Holy Spirit of the Almighty God (2 Corinthians 13:14).

Now let us journey with me back to the first family who were the first to experience the feeling of shame, fear, guilt, and the art of shifting blame. As we all know, the Garden story in Genesis chapters 2 and 3 started when Adam and Eve were in one accord with God. In the same way, when you and I enter this world, we are innocent because we do not know right from wrong. I believe if you or I were to die as a baby, we would all go to heaven. According to the scriptures, for sins to be fully evident in our lives, we must "repent and be baptized" (Acts 2:37–38). On that note, one can ask about a baby: What sins would a newborn have knowledge of committing that he or she would need to repent of and need the blood of Jesus to cleanse? I will let you ponder on that thought. One might argue the original sin theory. However, that would make God a liar, and

He is not (John 9:2–5, Ezekiel 18:19–32). Let us continue my spiritual transformation as God revealed things to me during my spiritual healing.

In Genesis 2:25, the scripture states, "They felt no shame." Everything was going well in the Garden for Adam and Eve until they allowed the devil to use them as a vessel to destroy God's wonderful creation, which is humankind. For many years, I read Genesis 3:1 and always thought the serpent was Satan until the spirit allowed me to read it through a different lens. The scripture says, "The serpent was craftier than any of the wild animals the Lord had made." Reading this scripture helped me to connect so many spiritual dots that God has allowed me to experience. Growing up as a child, I had witnessed the manifestation of the evil spirit taking over people's bodies to engage in different celebrations. Furthermore, as I study the spiritual realm, I have learned that whether it is God's Spirit or the adversary spirit, they need a vessel to dwell in. The serpent was already *crafty*. Another word for *crafty* is *sneaky*; the serpent was a perfect vessel for Satan to use as a tool to inflict shame through the disobedience of God in the lives of Adam and Eve, who started their spiritual journey as *shameless*.

In Genesis 3:8–13, we see how both Adam and Eve experienced shame and fear. After many years of God working through me, it has become evident that the people who hurt me (us) are in that craftiness bondage where Satan is ruling their mind, body, and soul to do his horrible deeds. Oftentimes, like Adam and Eve, my choosing to disobey God's Words or to have no desire to change and learn His ways leads me toward becoming readily available for Satan to dwell in. The devil is manifesting around us every day. There are many people who say Jesus is Lord, yet they continue to live in bondage because they have not "overcome the world" or laid their burdens down (1 John 5:4–5, Matthew 11:28–30). When we live in bondage, our focus is on the flesh and the tangible things that are seen; as a result, we are blinded from recognizing the real enemy, Satan (1 Peter 5:8–9). Consequently, we stay stuck in the flesh and never experience the true freedom that Jesus promised (Galatians 4:8–9, Galatians 5:1, John 8:36). When we are trapped in the flesh, we are more susceptible to hurting ourselves, other people, and carry the burden of hatred, bitterness, selfishness, unforgiveness, anger, etc. Furthermore, we become blind to the Words of God as truth because Jesus is either no longer enough, or we have no desire to know Him.

In Galatians 5:1, the Apostle Paul reminded us that Jesus died to set us free. Therefore, we should no longer be "burdened again by a yoke of slavery." I have been exposed to many painful experiences in my life; in my search for healing, I was faced with the decision to either allow my pain to become the master of my life by staying in bondage or allowing Jesus to become my master and be set free. My unwillingness to trust was a deficit in my life journey, which made it difficult for me to completely surrender to Jesus. I am so grateful that God has led me to choose Jesus and took Him at His Word like the desperate father whose son was dying and took Jesus at His Words (John 4:50). The story says the son was healed at the exact time that Jesus said, "Your son will live." I decided that I will no longer allow Satan's plan for my life to supersede God's original plan, which is for me to be set free (John 8:36). Satan may have tried to use his craftiness to make me believe that God inflicted me with all the awful experiences in my life, and I am not "fearfully and wonderfully made." I am choosing to believe He sacrificed His son in place of me because He loves me (John 3:16, 1 John 4:7–21, Isaiah 53:5–6).

I have accepted and embraced the fact that the people who have hurt me and will hurt me are not my enemies. God has made this revelation evident in my life through His grace as He opened my eyes to see the spiritual battle (Ephesians 6:12). In Revelation 12:12, when Satan was thrown down to earth and lost his privilege to have access to heaven, the scripture says,

> Therefore rejoice, you heavens and you who dwell in them! But woe to the earth and the sea because the devil has gone down to you! He is filled with fury because he knows that his time is short.

During my healing journey, the Holy Spirit compelled me to focus on the real enemy, Satan, and how he has waged war against our souls since the beginning of time. God revealing this message to me has allowed me to experience the peace and freedom that ignites in one's soul when you are set free from the burden of pain and hurt through forgiveness of self, and others, and loving the unlovable (Luke 6:32–36). I must note forgiveness does not mean disregarding or ignoring the fact that we were abused or hurt, and it does not mean there should not be any consequences for the abuser according to the law of the land (Genesis 3:14–15 and Galatians 6:7–10). I strive to remember when Jesus says in Matthew 6:15,

> But if you do not forgive others their sins, your
> Father will not forgive your sins.

There is no conditional option in this scripture, it is a direct warning. I often go back to another favorite passage of mine, Romans 5:8,

> But God demonstrates his own love for us in this:
> While we were still sinners, Christ died for us.

Whatever your chains or your shackles might be and as it may seem impossible, Jesus is ready to set you free like He has done for me or like He did for the man in Mark 5:8–13 or the woman who was subject to bleeding for many years in Matthew 9:20–25 or the lost son who returned home in Luke 15:11–31. Memories of my traumatic experiences did not go away and continue to be part of my journey as I yoke with Jesus. The difference in facing my thoughts and feelings with Jesus is that I am choosing daily to allow the Holy Spirit to be the queen of my chess game (life) by not allowing Satan's destructive plan to dictate the outcome of my soul's destination (Galatians 5:19–21, 2 Timothy 2:12, Matthew 6:14–15).

My prayer for God's daughters and sons is to decide to no longer allow Satan to paralyze us by becoming slaves to the trauma and tragedy that he has burdened our lives with. We cannot allow ourselves to be deceived by the power of delusion or believe the lies (2 Thessalonians 2:11–12; Luke 8:44) that our traumatic experiences define who we are as God's daughters! Jesus is ready to take our burdens and give us rest if we are willing to take Him at His word (Matthew 11:28–30, Hebrews 4:10–11).

Daughters and sons of God, let us not allow Satan's destructive plan to dictate the beginning and ending of our journey! Jesus took our *shame* on the cross so that we might choose Him. When tempted to believe Satan's lies, I remind myself that as long as I still breathe in this earthly tent, I am subject to the affliction of Satan (2 Corinthians 5:1–10). Those afflictions usually come in different forms, such as people, sickness, self-afflictions, confusion, division, etc. We must recognize who the real enemy is in this world, and he will not stop until Jesus comes back. Praise be to God through Jesus Christ; He has made the healing power available to anyone who accepts His spiritual gift in preparation for our new heavenly tent (body) by taking our sins on the cross. "He himself bore our sins" (1 Peter 2:24) in His body on the cross so that we might die to sins and live for righteousness; "by His wounds you have been healed." We are in a daily battle for our souls. Let us not become complacent and take our focus from our true enemy who has been working like a roaring lion since the Garden of Eden to separate us from the truth of God.

> Therefore, take up the whole armor of God, that you may be able to withstand in the evil day, and having done all, to stand firm. Stand therefore, having fastened on the belt of truth, and having put on the breastplate of righteousness, and, as shoes for your feet, having put on the readiness given by the gospel of peace. In all circumstances take up the shield of faith, with which you can extinguish all the flaming darts of the evil one; and take the helmet of salvation, and the sword of the Spirit, which is the word of God, praying at all times in the Spirit, with all prayer and supplication. (Ephesians 6:12–18 ESV)

The Desire to Know God

MOST PEOPLE IN the world identify themselves as *Christians*, while others identify themselves as *believers*. Those who walked with Jesus during His ministry were identified as Disciples. Although the word *Christian* is predominantly used to describe followers of Jesus throughout the world today, it was not commonly used during the early part of the first-century church. The word *Christian* was used later while Barnabas and Paul were teaching the people in Antioch (Acts 11:25–26). The name was given to them by the people they were teaching and simply means "Christ followers" or "Christlike." I believe whether you identify yourself as a Christian or a Disciple of Jesus Christ, the expectation for all of us is the same according to Scriptures because you are claiming Jesus as your Rabbi, Master, Lord, and Teacher. For example, I identify myself as a *Disciple* of Jesus Christ. Carrying the identity of a Disciple of Jesus reminds me to remain sober in my desire to be a student seeking to understand the intimate parts of His heart. As the Apostle Paul so eloquently reminds us in Philippians 3:10–11, when I made the decision to become Jesus's Disciple, I renounced everything that I was to be molded through the power given in His death to reach fullness in Christ at the last resurrection.

> Yes, I gave it all up in order to know Him, that
> is, to know the power of His resurrection and
> the fellowship of His sufferings as I am being
> conformed to His death so that somehow I
> might arrive at being resurrected from the dead.
> (Philippians 3:10–11 CJB)

In my search for a deeper relationship with Jesus as a young thirteen-year-old girl, I had the opportunity to explore and spend time with different religious groups. I thank God every day for exposing me to them because those experiences led me to grow deeper in my convictions about Jesus. The one conviction I gained during my time in these different faith-based churches is that religion is Satan's biggest weapon to divide God's church. We must remember that God's church is much bigger than any earthly denomination.

In my walk with Jesus, I have had several personal encounters with Him that have guided me in my walk with God. During my time at these faith-based churches, I recall their organizational structure was guided by their interpretation of the scriptures. As a result, they often missed the heart of God as they selected parts of the scriptures that matched their doctrine. Despite it all, God used each of them to help me grow in my spiritual journey.

In my initial walk with God, I identified myself as a Christian or a believer. I had prayed Jesus into my heart. I had a personal healing encounter with Jesus (a story for another devotion). I was baptized (submerged in water) and had the confidence that God had forgiven my sins; I was chosen, and He rescued me. I was deeply religious, and many of my friends in school called me *good girl* or *sweet girl*. My family called me crazy Annaika. I knew and memorized many scriptures and became a prayer warrior. I went to church on Sundays, Wednesdays, and Fridays. I often invited my friends to church and talked to people about Jesus. Wow! I felt rather good; that was a great resume to have as a teenager. Well! That is far from the truth.

At some point in my journey, God's Spirit allowed me to feel like I was missing something. My spirit started to feel troubled. I started asking myself: What is my purpose as a soldier in God's army on this earth? I started questioning why I had all this scripture-based knowledge yet felt empty. I started saying, "There has got to be more than being a grateful saved sinner." I began praying for God to show me the next step in my life.

Now that I look back, I can clearly see I was a hearer of the Word and partially a doer of the Word. In addition, I lacked the complete surrender to the Holy Spirit's Lordship that would transform me into the ambassador that Jesus called me out of the darkness to become (2 Corinthians 5:11–21, James 1:22–25). I am incredibly grateful for the Redeeming Love Christian Church in Nanuet, New York, that God used to teach me the fundamentals of my faith that led me to my deep convictions about Jesus, the power of prayer, and the power of the manifestation of the Holy Spirit in my life.

Having the knowledge of the Bible gave me a form of godliness, but not knowing how to utilize that godliness in every area of my life, denied me the transforming power of the Word of God (Ephesians 4:20–24, 2 Timothy 3:5). I was being a "good Christian girl" and a "good person" in the eyes of the world. Like many of us, I was extremely comfortable with Jesus being my Savior because He rescued me, yet His lordship over my life was lacking.

I honestly believe it is in our nature to embrace the need for a Savior because there is so much we need to be rescued from. That is why John 3:16 is immensely popular and acceptable to the Christian world. However, the lordship of Jesus is seen as optional because we love our *right* to do what we want, or feel is right to do. So we say Jesus is Lord, yet we let the world form the standard that we live by. Furthermore, those of us who read or know the scriptures often use them to make our points instead of allowing the Truth of God through the Holy Spirit to lead us. if you wonder what example I have to clarify my statement above, look around you at what has been happening over the past four years (2020–2024). The comments and actions that I saw those who call themselves Christian/Disciples of Jesus Christ making—which I believe are contrary to what the Word of God teaches—trouble my inner soul. My comfort in all this is that Jesus will judge each of us for every careless word or deed we have spewed (Matthew 12:33–37).

In Acts 2:36 (CJB), when Peter addressed the crowd, he exclaimed: "Therefore, let the whole house of Israel know beyond doubt that God has made him both Lord and Messiah——this Yeshua, whom you executed on a stake!" What does it mean for someone to be Lord? The word *Lord* in Hebrew-Greek is *kurios* (pronunciation: Koo-ree-os) derived from another Hebrew-Greek word *kuros*, which stands for supremacy, supreme in authority; as a noun: controller, might, power master owner, etc. (*Hebrew-Greek Key Word Study Bible* definition).

As you are submerged under the water, symbolizing dying to your old self/sinful nature (Romans 6:1–7), you are declaring that Jesus is your Master, and you are His servant. As you read the word *servant*, your mind might automatically translate the word servant to *slave*. The reality is, my friend, whether you admit it or not, each of us is a slave to something or someone in our lives. Nonetheless, as Paul reminds us in Romans 6:16–18, we each have a choice. We must decide if we are a slave to sin, which will lead us to death, or to the obedience of God, which will lead us to righteousness. When you and I said Jesus is Lord during our baptism, our allegiance at that moment was given to Jesus Christ. Our allegiance is not to our upbringing values, our family, our opinions, our political party affiliation, our country/flag, our job/career, the worldly pleasure; you fill in the blank.

God's Holy Spirit that is living in me willed me to cry out to Jehovah for more purpose due to my gratitude for what Jesus did for me. The Holy Spirit opened my mind and heart to see how just knowing the scriptures and quoting them was fulfilling in some way, but empty. I was being robbed of the freedom that having Jesus as Lord in every area of my life was able to give me (Galatians 5:1). I carried unforgiveness, fits of rage, slander, lying, ungratefulness, conceitedness, love of self, boasting, hatred, and disobedience for a period during my Christian walk. You might say, "Well, you were not a Christian!" Before you are quick to condemn me, you must reflect on your own life at this moment; can you say you are free from sins? Even the most devout Christian/Disciple among us is burdened with sins (John 8:7, Romans 3:23–24). We are all a work in progress in our journey with Jesus until we receive our heavenly body. We must work out our salvation daily as we allow the Holy Spirit to convict us toward holiness (Philippians 2:12–13, 2 Corinthians 10:1–10, Revelation 21:1–4).

What I have learned thus far in my journey with Jesus is that most Christians/Disciples are still in bondage because we think that knowing the scriptures, teaching, and preaching them are the main sources of our deliverance. Jesus in his ministry asked us to bring our burden to Him (Matthew 11:28). Despite knowing what His Word says, we continue to carry the shame, guilt, and powerless spirit that Satan has imported into our lives to destroy our soul (2 Corinthians 4:4, 2 Corinthians 2:10–11, 1 Peter 5:8, Luke 22:31).

I often hear people saying, "I know what the scripture says. I desire to do it, but I find myself having a hard time following through with what the scripture says." Does that statement remind you of someone in the Bible (Romans 7:15)? The writer of Hebrews went further, making the argument, if we claim to know Christ Jesus, and we continue to sin, there is no sacrifice left (Hebrews 10:26). The writer in 1 John 3:6 went even further to tell us we do not know Christ if we continue sinning after we claim to remain in Him. Believe me, I hated my sins and cried often for God to take them away as a young Christian. In my cries to the Lord, He opened my eyes to see clearly why I am free yet living in bondage. I simply thought that I could set myself free by being a doer of the Word of God and knowing the scriptures, which are all important according to Jesus (John 12:47, Luke 10:16, Luke 6:49).

My complete healing came when I decided to let the Holy Spirit of God who lives in me become Lord of my life through Jesus Christ, who is my Master. The key to my deliverance was when I decided to surrender and learned that I could not save myself. Although I said Jesus is Lord and my Savior, I was still holding on to so much garbage that I allowed the adversary (Satan) to torment my spirit and interfere with my effort to serve God. Therefore, I never entered Jesus's complete rest (Hebrews 4:9–10). This revelation led me to forgiving myself and many people in my life, and my attitude toward repentance when I hear the Word of God is different.

> Do not let sin control the way you live; do not
> give in to sinful desires. (Romans 6:12 NLT)

As someone who has experienced God's grace and mercy in so many different areas in life, I believe we struggle to allow the Word of God to transform us because we try to fix things ourselves. The task of trying to free yourself from sin is exhausting and burdensome; that is why only Jesus can fix it. Jesus is our high priest who came to destroy Satan's plan by taking our iniquities upon himself because in our human flesh, we just cannot do it (Hebrews 4:14–16; Isaiah 53:6). God has tried to use human beings for many centuries, and each time we fail miserably. Spend some time reading the Old Testament to learn about God's multiple efforts to use humankind as His voice to turn us from our wicked ways. Many times, I hear preachers preaching about repentance of sins, but they have fallen short in teaching people they can only have victory over sin by allowing the Holy Spirit to carve out whatever the cancer (sins) in their lives might be.

If we could do it on our own, Jesus would have left us with just the Word (Bible); instead, He sent us the counselor to make His Word alive in us by guiding us to all truth (John 16:13). In my distress, the Spirit of God reminded me of my first encounter with God and led me to cry to the Lord for answers; He heard my cry and led me to the next level of my spiritual journey. In Matthew 7:7–8, Jesus says,

> Ask and it will be given to you; seek and you
> will find; knock and the door will be opened to
> you. For everyone who asks receives; the one who
> seeks finds, and to the one who knocks, the door
> will be opened.

If you read my *first encounter* with Jesus, you know He did not just hear me, but He came and gave me a new purpose.

At the age of sixteen, during the period of my cry to seek God deeper, I was invited to a Valentine's dance party that was being hosted by the Hudson Valley Church of Christ. My initial religious reaction was to judge. I wondered what kind of Christians these people are, who are dancing. I did attend the party, and to my surprise, the party blew my mind as I witnessed a group of people gathering, having fun with respect, and no inappropriate behavior.

The women from the party invited me to worship with them, and I attended their worship service two weeks later. A member from their congregation who lived near my house picked me up and took me to the service. Following the worship service, they invited me to a café for lunch, and this is where I clearly saw what I was missing in my walk with Jesus. I recalled one sister confessed to two other sisters some deep shortcoming sins that she engaged in during the week (James 5:16). After witnessing the women using the Holy Scriptures to remind their sister of God's love, grace, and expectation as a Disciple of Jesus Christ, I thought to myself, *These women applied what they are reading to change their lives!* I knew at that moment why the Spirit allowed me to feel the void in my inner soul.

When the sisters from lunch asked me, "Would you like to study the Bible?" In my pride, I said, "I know the Bible; just tell me how to apply it." In their humility, they explained they would rather I learn it from Jesus. How could I argue with learning from Jesus? Their approach reminded me of how Paul addressed the religious people from Athens (Acts 17:22–30) because the sisters met me where I was spiritually.

The decision to become Jesus's student (Disciple) by allowing the Bible to be living and active in my life, along with the foundation that God laid for me, has been the fuel that the Holy Spirit needed to purify me inside and out. I was very comfortable using the Word of God to help others but did not often apply it to my own life. I knew becoming a doer of the Word of God in my personal life was evident because my family and friends were critical of the changes in my life. Satan used many of them to become obstacles in my journey.

I must also confess that as I allowed the Word of God to transform my inner soul, my family and friends were not the only obstacles in my path. I also became my own enemy, fighting God for many years to forgive those who had caused me physical and emotional pain. Glory be to God, if you read my devotional titled *The Battle for Our Soul*, you know that the adversary (Satan) tried to win, but God prevailed.

My question for you today, as you assess your walk with Jesus, is this: is Hebrews 4:12 "For the word of God is alive and active. Sharper than any double-edged sword, it penetrates even to dividing soul and spirit, joints and marrow; it judges the thoughts and attitudes of the heart" evident in your personal life? For those of you who have been in the army of God, you may say being a doer of the Word does not necessarily mean you are walking in step with the Spirit of God; I agree with you more than you know. Being a Christian, a Disciple of Jesus Christ, is a way of life, not a matter of doing. Our motive for why we follow Jesus matters. Our decision to follow Jesus is personal. Jesus will never force you to love Him. If that were His intention, I believe as the voice of God, He could have stopped Adam and Eve from choosing darkness.

I became a doer because Jesus first loved me, and I responded to His love with the desire to be like Him in my gratitude for rescuing me. I have chosen to become a slave in God's eternal kingdom. If you are obeying and/or becoming a doer of the Word of God because of guilt, fear, for people, for show, or just because, you will be burdened, you will feel empty at some point, you will feel fake, and you might even walk away from His love and grace. Our survival as a Christian/Disciple depends on the foundation that we build in our journey with Jesus (Matthew 13:1–23). I have also learned, basing your Christianity on others' faith is a dangerous path because people will disappoint you, but Jesus never will (Romans 5:5–21).

In His explanation of expectation for those who choose Him as their Rabbi, Jesus utilizes the statement "whoever wants to be" to reinforce, we each have a choice and if we choose Him, we no longer live for this world but for His purpose (Matthew 16:24–27).

CHAPTER 4

God's Heart

For this is what the LORD says: "I will extend peace to her like a river, and the wealth of nations like a flooding stream; you will nurse and be carried on her arm and dandled on her knees. As a mother comforts her child, so will I comfort you; and you will be comforted over Jerusalem." (Isaiah 66:12–13 NIV)

If my people, who are called by my name, shall humble themselves, and pray, and seek my face, and turn from their wicked ways; then will I hear from heaven, and will forgive their sin, and will heal their land. (2 Chronicle 7:14 ASV)

God's voice thunders in marvelous ways; he does great things beyond our understanding. He says to the snow, "Fall on the earth," and to the rain shower, "Be a mighty downpour." So that everyone he has made may know his work, he stops all people from their labor. (Job 37:5–7 NIV)

> For the Son of Man came to seek and to save the
> lost. (Luke 19:10 ESV)

HAVE YOU EVER had moments reading a scripture that you have read in the past and on a particular day, reading it again seems like you have never read it before? It always amazes me that no matter how many times I read a scripture or passage, God always reveals a new applicable lesson to my life. However, 1 John 4:7–21 seems to always be consistent each time I read it, "God is love." The writer wrote the word love twenty-four times (NIV) to help us understand that God is love and to tell us if we claim to know Him and have no love, we are liars. The love that the writer is describing is known in Hebrew-Greek as *agapao*, to love in a social or moral standard. That love is different from the love that derives from the Hebrew-Greek word *phileo*, which connects to feelings or expressions. For example, in Matthew 10:37 Jesus used the word *Phileo*. Jesus is saying our affection for Him as our God/Lord/Savior/Redeemer must supersede all emotional connection that we have for our family. For us to better understand the gift of love given to us through Jesus Christ, we must go back to Genesis 6 to understand its significance. God's voice in the flesh, willingly stooped down to the lowest level so that we can have the incredible invitation to share in His kingdom's blessings.

> The Lord saw how great the wickedness of the human race had become on the earth, and that every inclination of the thoughts of the human heart was only evil all the time. The Lord regretted that he had made human beings on the earth, and his heart was deeply troubled. So the Lord said, "I will wipe from the face of the earth the human race I have created—and with them the animals, the birds and the creatures that move along the ground—for I regret that I have made them." But Noah found favor in the eyes of the Lord. (Genesis 6:5–8 NIV)

ADONAI saw that the people on earth were very wicked, that all the imaginings of their heart were always of evil only. ADONAI regretted that he had made humankind on the earth; it grieved his heart. ADONAI said, "I will wipe out humankind, whom I have created, from the whole earth; and not only human beings, but animals, creeping things and birds in the air; for I regret that I ever made them. But Noach found grace in the sight of ADONAI." (CJB)

As I meditate while reading these scriptures, I am in awe of how much God so deeply loves us. He is always looking for the one righteous person who is willing to love Him above all. As a parent, I can relate to the pain that God felt as He watched His children, human creation, choose Satan's voice to follow; they chose to allow Satan's spirit to dwell in them. God concluded that every tendency of His children was evil. The scripture states that God was deeply troubled/grieved by what He saw. The word *grieve* in the Hebrew-Greek language is *atsab* (pronunciation: *aw-tsab*), which describes physical and emotional pain and anguish that one can experience. God was in so much agony watching humankind destroying their souls; He saw them as irreparable and resolved one decision, destruction.

I know God does not take any pleasure in watching us use our free will to do harm to ourselves and others because He says so. In Ezekiel 18:23 (NLT), God says,

> Do you think that I like to see wicked people die?
> says the Sovereign LORD. Of course not! I want
> them to turn from their wicked ways and live.

God's deep desire has always been for us to simply turn from our wicked ways and come back to Him. I have always wondered during the four-hundred-year period of God's spiritual silence until the arrival of Jesus, what was God like in heaven? I picture Him grieving the continuous disregard for His law and the constant rejection from humankind. I also envision Him pacing back and forth in His kingdom saying to Himself, "I cannot do this again. I can't destroy them again!" Yes, indeed, He did promise that He would never destroy life by waters again (Genesis 9:11), but there are so many other ways He could have chosen to destroy us.

I also picture the joy in His heart as His voice whispered, "Send Me. Maybe, just maybe, if we demonstrate to them how to draw closer to us (Father-Son-Holy Spirit) instead of telling them, they might come back to us." I also envision God with extraordinary joy saying, "Yes, let us take the sins of the whole world and die in their place so that I, their Creator, can also be their rescuer if they choose me." I truly believe John 3:16, "For God so Loved the world that he gave his one and only son, that whoever believes in him shall not perish but have eternal Life," was possibly written on the day in heaven that God decided to give us all one more chance to be reunited with Him through Jesus Christ, who became the Bible in action (John 1:14).

In my early Christian walk, Romans 10:9–11 was taught to me as the path to Jesus. In part, the people who taught me the scriptures were right! However, as God allowed me to study the Bible for myself, I learned through scriptures that the writer in the book of Romans was speaking about faith in Jesus, which was taken out of context regarding Salvation. These scriptures are also some of the most used scriptures in the religious world that are often used to deceive many people into believing that "confessing Jesus with your mouth" will grant you Salvation. In verse 14 of the same chapter 10, the writer made it noticeably clear that you must know Jesus to believe. Yes, declaring "Jesus is Lord" and believing in His resurrection are fundamental to our faith in the path toward salvation. However, according to the Messiah's own words, confessing and immersing in the water of baptism are both important to be a born-again Christian. Jesus replied,

> "Very truly I tell you, no one can see the kingdom of God unless they are born again." "How can someone be born when they are old?"

Nicodemus asked. "Surely they cannot enter a second time into their mother's womb to be born!" Jesus answered, "Very truly I tell you, no one can enter the kingdom of God unless they are born of water and the Spirit. Flesh gives birth to flesh, but the Spirit gives birth to spirit. You should not be surprised at my saying, 'You must be born again.' The wind blows wherever it pleases. You hear its sound, but you cannot tell where it comes from or where it is going. So it is with everyone born of the Spirit." (John 3:1–8)

Jesus Himself, as the Messiah, modeled for us the incredible process that He preached by His own example in Matthew 3:13–16,

Then Jesus came from Galilee to the Jordan to be baptized by John. But John tried to deter him, saying, "I need to be baptized by you, and do you come to me?" Jesus replied, "Let it be so now; it is proper for us to do this to fulfill all righteousness." Then John consented. As soon as Jesus was baptized, he went up out of the water. At that moment heaven was opened, and he saw the Spirit of God descending like a dove and alighting on him.

If Jesus can say he must be baptized to "fulfill all righteousness," how can we disregard the power that comes through repentance, confessing Jesus is Lord, and being baptized (submerged) which symbolizes the new life that Jesus promises us (Acts 2:37–41)? Colossians 2:11–12 (CJB) and many other scriptures describe for us the power of dying to our old selves in baptism and rising into a new life just as Christ was raised from the dead to "wipe away the bill of charge against us." There are many characteristics I learned about Jesus in His ministry, but the one trait I have always loved about Him is that He never asks us to do anything that He Himself has not demonstrated. In the same way, His Apostles started the first-century church with the same response that the Messiah has taught them,

> Now when they heard this, they were pricked in their heart, and said unto Peter and to the rest of the apostles, Men and brethren, what shall we do? Then Peter said unto them, Repent, and be baptized every one of you in the name of Jesus Christ for the remission of sins, and ye shall receive the gift of the Holy Ghost. For the promise is unto you, and to your children, and to all that are afar off, even as many as the Lord our God shall call. And with many other words did he testify and exhort, saying, "Save yourselves from this untoward generation." (Acts 2:37–40 KJV)

I am not writing this to disprove or disqualify anyone's faith in Jesus Christ. I am a prime example of how, in my deep desire to learn about Jesus, He reveals Himself to me by using diverse congregations to influence my walk with Him. I prayed Jesus into my heart and confessed Him as my Savior on several occasions; however, I learned the true power that I was seeking is hidden in dying to myself and being raised into a new creation with the Holy Spirit of God as my Counselor in baptism (Galatians 2:20, 2 Corinthians 5:17–21, Isaiah 43:18–21, Romans 8:11–17, etc.). Yes, believing and confessing with your mouth that Jesus is Lord is a positive step toward a relationship with Him, but according to Scriptures, there is more to the process of becoming a new creation in Christ Jesus as a Christian/Disciple. I would encourage anyone who is seeking a deeper understanding of God to read the Holy Scriptures, and spend time with Jesus to learn how you can enter His kingdom. Do not take my words, your preachers' words, your parents' words, and/or any outside influence; kneel before His throne and learn from Him through the Holy Scriptures. Jesus tells us He is the bread of life that gives everlasting food and drink (John 6:35). In the same chapter of John 6:63, Jesus addressed the Disciples that were with Him, saying,

> The Spirit gives life; the flesh counts for nothing.
> The words I have spoken to you—they are full of
> the Spirit and Life.

We should be so grateful to know that Jesus did not come to condemn us. He simply came to give us life and a new beginning with our maker. I have contemplated this thought for a while. If God wanted to condemn us, why would He need to come to us? As you meditate on this thought, think of everything that God has allowed or caused in the Old and New Testaments. Why would He need to send Jesus His *Word* in the flesh to condemn or punish us? Jesus came with one purpose: that is to seek and save His lost children who are lost in the scheme of Satan's lies (Luke 19:9–10). Jesus was clear about His purpose on earth during His ministry. When they came to arrest Jesus, He made it very clear that God could rescue Him if that was the plan.

> "Put your sword back in its place," Jesus said to him. "For all who draw the sword will die by the sword. Are you not aware that I can call on My Father, and He will at once put at My disposal more than twelve legions of angels? But how then would the Scriptures be fulfilled that say it must happen this way?" (Matthew 26:53 BSB)

God never makes a decision in vain; His heart is to rescue every soul on this earth, but He also knows many will reject Him and will choose the wicked path (Matthew 7:13–14). Even though God knew a few would find His path, He felt that the few were worthy of His grace and mercy. Jesus says there is a gate and a path to eternal life, and He is the way (John 14:6–7, Revelation 1:17–18). Many people often wonder, *How do we find the path to eternal life? What does it mean to believe and love God?* In my walk with Jesus, I have learned one important fact about God through the Holy Scriptures: He will never leave us in the dark. Scriptures clearly depict His expectation to *whoever* says yes to His reconciliation invitation (2 Corinthians 5:19–21). Through different series of devotions, we will explore what it means to *believe* and *love* God according to Jesus's own words and actions.

CHAPTER 5

Jesus Is God the Messiah: Part I

Introduction

GROWING UP AS a child, I learned about Jesus through the religious school that I attended. Unfortunately, I recall learning more about the significance of Jesus's mother, Mary, instead of Jesus at an early age. Indeed, I believe Mary, the mother of Jesus, is an earthly, significant part of His existence. In fact, the scriptures tell us that she was highly favored by God (Luke 1:28). However, as I grew older, I began to question, "Who is this Jesus?" God allowed my curiosity to be nurtured through both trials and victories. In John 14:6, Jesus declared, "I am the way and the truth and the life. No one comes to the Father except through me." Jesus's message in this scripture, I believe, answers a fundamental question that is often asked: What is the path to God's eternal glory? I often hear the statement, "There are many ways to God."

During Jesus's ministry, He was very plain in His answer about how we get to God. As we study Jesus's ministry, we will read about His clear understanding that people would reject His sacrificial act to bring us back to God. I believe Jesus's statement in the passage above was absolute and with authority. He left no room for doubt or confusion. I have always asked myself, and I would like to pose to you, as you join me in this journey, these questions: Do you want to find "the path" to God our Creator? (He is the way.) Do you want "the truth"? (He is the truth.) Do you want "the life"? (He is the life.) Yes, I do believe that Jesus is the only way to the physical and spiritual reconnection that we all so desire with God, which was tarnished in the Garden of Eden (Genesis 3:1–24). I believe with absolute confidence that He is the only way to God because my life is a testimony that Jesus is the only life that keeps my heart beating in a world that is so spiritually empty of truth.

In this ministry, we will study Jesus through scriptures and applicable life experiences that will, prayerfully, give you some insight into who this Jesus is. Although I may reference points from different spiritual warriors whom Jesus has utilized to impact my life, most of the insights shared will be from the Holy Scriptures in the Bible. I will also use different Bible versions, including Greek/Hebrew Bibles, to study the scriptures.

Jesus, the Father, and the Holy Spirit are one.

When you hear "the Father, the Son, and the Holy Spirit," what comes to your mind?

When I hear the Trinity—Father, Son, and the Holy Spirit—I think of my life. For example, I am Annaika; there is only one of me. However, even though I am one person, I have different roles and attributes such as being a Disciple of Jesus Christ, a mother, a wife, a friend, etc. These roles that I carry out for different purposes do not change the fact that I am Annaika. I see the Trinity the same way, as the Father, the Son, and the Holy Spirit are all one higher power (God) that have distinct functions for different purposes.

In John 1:1–18, the beautiful work of the Trinity is described.

In verses 1–3 from the book of John, the writer brought to our attention the truth about God's Word:

> In the beginning was the Word, and the Word was with God, and the Word was God. He was with God in the beginning. Through him all things were made; without him nothing was made that has been made.

As we dive into this incredible puzzle of who Jesus is, let us ponder for a moment Genesis 1:1–5:

> In the beginning God created the heavens and the earth. Now the earth was formless and empty, darkness was over the surface of the deep, and the spirit of God was hovering over the waters. And God said, "Let there be light," and there was light. God saw that the light was good, and he separated the light from the darkness. God called the light "day," and the darkness he called "night." And there was evening, and there was morning—the first day.

John chapter 1 is drawing our attention to the fact that Jesus was present when God created the world. You may wonder, as you read Genesis, that God and the Spirit were there, but there was no mention of Jesus, the Son. I would like to draw your attention back to Genesis chapter 1, and as you read it, count how many times God spoke the world into existence. I counted thirteen times (NIV) when God spoke the creation of the world into existence. Keep this thought in mind as we go back to John chapter 1.

Jesus Is God the Messiah: Part 2

Jesus Is God!
Part 2

In the beginning was the Word, and the Word was with God, and the Word was God. He was with God in the beginning. Through him all things were made; without him nothing was made that has been made. In him was life, and that life was the light of all mankind. The light shines in the darkness, and the darkness has not overcome it. There was a man sent from God whose name was John. He came as a witness to testify concerning that light, so that through him all might believe. He himself was not the light; he came only as a witness to the light. The true light that gives light to everyone was coming into the world. He was in the world, and though the world was made through him, the world did not recognize him. He came to that which was his own, but his own did not receive him. Yet to all who did receive him, to those who believed in his name, he gave the right to become children of

God—children born not of natural descent, nor of human decision or a husband's will, but born of God. The Word became flesh and made his dwelling among us. We have seen his glory, the glory of the one and only Son, who came from the Father, full of grace and truth. (John 1:1–14 NIV)

Let us follow the sequence of events **that Apostle John** is bringing to our attention:

1. The Word was there in the beginning.
2. The Word was with God in the beginning.
3. The Word was God.
4. The same was true in the beginning with God.
5. All things were made by Him and without Him, nothing was made.

Let us pause for a moment: *what just happened?* The writer was talking about the *Word* (noun) and changed it to *Him* (pronoun). The writer changed the *Word* that was present in the beginning to a specific living being and described the function of that living being.

- In Him was life.
- His life was the light of men.
- His light shines in darkness, but the darkness does not understand Him.
- He was the true light that gave light to everyone entering the world. God, the Creator of the world, came into the world, and the world did not know Him.
- Not even His own people recognized Him.
- He gave everyone who believed and received Him the right to become children of God. *What does it mean to believe and receive Him?* We will explore this question later in writing.
- The Word became flesh and made His dwelling among us.
- He came full of grace and mercy.

I am certain and hopeful that as you are reading the Scriptures, you are beginning to see how Jesus is the architect and builder of the world because when He walked on earth, He was the very *Word* of God in flesh. He, the *Word*! The *Word* became a verb in the physical form to demonstrate to us how to live the words of God in our lives. The *Word* (Jesus) is the cells, ligaments, and bones that God used to create the world into existence. When Jesus (Yeshua—Hebrew name for Jesus) says in John 12:48, "There is a judge for the one who rejects me and does not accept my words; the very words I have spoken will condemn them at the last day," He is simply warning us that the Son—who represents the physical form of the Word of God—will actually be our Judge because He is God. Jesus says again in John 10:30, "I and the Father are one." He is declaring that He is God, and rightfully so. The Father, the Son, and the Holy Spirit are one God!

For one to say they believe in God and reject the Son, who is the Word of God in action (1 John 2:23), or the Holy Spirit, who is our counselor and the spiritual passageway of communication between us and God (Romans 8:26–27), their worship is in vain. Jesus is clear, as we read earlier, Yeshua is the only way to the Father. Lastly, Jesus's appearance to John in Revelation 1:17–18, where He exclaimed, "Don't be afraid! I am the First and the Last. The living One. I was dead, but look! I am alive forever and ever! And I hold the keys to death and Sheol (Hades)," is a clear warning to us all that accepting His final effort as Jesus the Messiah to unite us with Him as we were once before is the final preparation for the last judgment that is to come.

Jesus, the Messiah, is the vocal voice of the living God. God Himself became flesh to exemplify how to live under His vocal authority. The voice of God (Jesus in spiritual form) had to return where He belongs after He died for me and you (John 14:27–28). He knew that without a spiritual connection with Him, we would get lost trying to follow His Words; therefore, He sent us the Holy Scriptures as our map to get to Him. That is why Jesus's teaching in John 16:1–15 was so important for Him to explain to His Disciples.

The Holy Spirit, whom Jesus identifies as our counselor, is the compass given by God to those who say yes to His voice. The Spirit leads us to God as we live the Holy Scriptures in our lives like Jesus demonstrated for us (John 16:13). Just as Jesus became the Word in flesh when we declare that Jesus is Lord during baptism, and we're submerged under the water (died to the old self) and raised out of the water as a symbol of the new creation (Romans 6:4), we as Disciples of Jesus Christ become God's temple because God's Spirit lives in us. Yes, Jesus died for everyone in the world (John 3:16), but He also knows not everyone will say yes to Him because they love darkness instead of light (John 3:19–21). Yes, God Himself, through Jesus Christ, came into this world in human flesh full of "grace and mercy."

Similarly, while He was living in human flesh, He was faced with choices like you and me. Satan knew Jesus was only the vocal part of God; therefore, Satan also knew Jesus could choose to disobey God's voice while in the flesh. As we learned in (Matthew 4:1–11), Satan tried to manipulate Jesus to disobey the voice of God. Just as Adam and Eve (Genesis 1–2) had a personal relationship with God in the Garden of Eden and were able to hear and see God in their presence, Jesus likewise had a personal relationship with God when He was in the flesh. The difference between Jesus and Adam and Eve is that Jesus did not allow the flesh, which is our sinful nature (Galatians 5:16–21), to destroy God's original plan to be one with us for eternity (Colossians 2:14; 1 Peter 2:24–25). Adam and Eve were faced with a choice (Genesis 3:1–7) in the same way Jesus did in Matthew 4:1–11; they chose to allow the voice of God to diminish and the voice of Satan to increase, which led to our separation from God (Genesis 3). In contrast, Jesus had a choice and chose to reject the voice of Satan and allowed the voice of God that lives in His human flesh to be the bridge that unites us with the fullness of God once again (John 14:6; Romans 6:5–7).

As we ponder on our free will to choose the destiny of our lives like Adam, Eve, and Jesus, which voice are we listening to? The option is simple: we either listen to the voice of God or the devil.

What compass are you and I using to guide our lives, God or the devil? The reality is that each compass leads our soul to a destination, whether you admit to this truth or not (Matthew 7:13–14). Jesus came and lived His life demonstrating what the writer of Hebrews is compelling us to look like if we choose Jesus and the Holy Spirit as our compass:

> For the word of God is alive and active. Sharper than any double-edged sword, it penetrates even to dividing soul and spirit, joints and marrow; it judges the thoughts and attitudes of the heart. Nothing in all creation is hidden from God's sight. Everything is uncovered and laid bare before the eyes of him to whom we must give account. (Hebrews 4:12–13 NIV)

This passage is a reminder that the Word of God and the Holy Spirit of God—who Jesus promises lives in us (John 14:16; John 16:13; John 3:8)—is our compass; therefore, our lives have a different purpose.

I work in the cancer world, which gives me a simple analogy to what the Word of God and the Holy Spirit can do if we allow Him to remove sins in our lives that often paralyze us. As we read in the Scriptures (Psalm 139; Hebrews 4:13), God already knows everything about each of our lives, so why not give Him a chance to restore you? I know that the words of God are continuing to remove and repair so many cancer cells (sins) in my life. My life is also proof of what He can do when we decide to return to Him and allow Him to be the continuous spiritual radiation to heal our inner soul from Satan's lies and schemes that are killing us. Yes, just as radiation causes scars and sometimes lifelong pain, as we repent from our sins and change our lives, there will be scars and long-term impacts. God promises to free us from our sins, but He never says the consequences of our sins will be wiped out. The Word of God without the manifestation of the Holy Spirit will seem powerless in our lives. Jesus says in John 14:16–17,

> If you love me, keep my command. And I will ask
> the Father, and He will give you another advocate
> to help you and be with you forever—the Spirit
> of truth.

As you continue this journey with me, I will share with you my own encounter with Jesus and how He continues to penetrate my soul, dividing spirit, joints, marrow, and the battles in my mind which, if allowed, will and have created cancer cells (sins) in my heart.

I pray these devotionals expand your mind to think about your life as you decide who will be the master of your life. Yes, we have free will, but we must choose wisely because there is a cost for each choice that we make. The result of your choice determines the destination of your soul. Take heed to Jesus's words from John 12:48,

> There is a judge for the one who rejects me and
> does not accept my words; the very words I have
> spoken will condemn them at the last day.

CHAPTER 7

Praising God through Chronic Pain

Therefore, in order to keep me from becoming conceited, I was given a thorn in my flesh, a messenger of Satan, to torment me. Three times I pleaded with the Lord to take it away from me. But He said to me, "My grace is sufficient for you, for my power is made perfect in weakness." Therefore, I will boast all the more gladly about my weaknesses, so that Christ's power may rest on me. That is why, for Christ's sake, I delight in weaknesses, in insults, in hardships, in persecutions, in difficulties. For when I am weak, then I am strong. (2 Corinthians 12:7–10 NIV)

IMAGINE WAKING UP most days feeling like needles are pricking you all over your body, while your bones feel like wires or three-string cords that are being twisted to make a rope! Imagine waking up most days relying on God to be your strength by praying you can make it through the day! Imagine being awake but not able to get up from the bed because your body is fighting against your will to get going! Imagine, after fighting through the physical pain all day, where your brain feels exhausted, where you cannot recall simple things or the names of your friends and family, even though you are looking at them! Imagine feeling like bugs are running under your skin like an electricity wave! Imagine having a full-blown flare of the symptoms mentioned above, where your body is retaliating for pushing through as your toes, legs, hands, back, eyes, and your muscles/bones start twitching and folding. Your loved ones can visibly see your body in crisis while you are screaming and crying, and there is nothing they can do to help! Imagine driving home from work or other places, praying to God that your legs don't start twitching/folding because you know your survival and others' on the road depends on it! Imagine your body feels beat up when talking, breathing, reading, and walking, becomes exceedingly difficult! Imagine your vision gets blurry, and you feel like your sight is diminishing slowly while experiencing extreme fatigue!

As you are reading and imagining the description above, you may think this person must be depressed, with a limited social life, on a lot of medication, or must be bitter. Well, that is far from the truth because I am that person. Yes, there are good days amidst this horror when I feel ready to conquer the world, but at any second—without any warning—the pain starts again.

For many years, several medical tests have been completed to detect different diseases, and praise God, all tests have been negative. The symptoms mimic several different types of debilitating illnesses that I am grateful to be free from. Consequently, fibromyalgia was the final diagnosis given to me by doctors since there is no other known medical reason that they could find. In my search for answers, four years ago, I was given the diagnosis of benign fasciculation syndrome, which matches some of my symptoms but does not provide me any concrete answers. Since there is no cure for my symptoms, I have been prescribed pain medications that, over the years, I have elected not to take. They make me feel mentally disconnected, and for me, that is worse than the physical pain. Nonetheless, pain medication does work for others, and people should take them if needed to relieve their pain. I believe the knowledge in the medical world is given by God to help us while we are living in this decaying body.

In my journey with chronic pain, I can connect, to some extent, to the Apostle Paul in 2 Corinthians 12:7–10. Although I have not experienced anywhere near what he went through for the sake of his faith in Christ, I have pleaded with God to take this chronic pain away, and I am choosing to believe that, for my benefit, He says no. Knowing myself, I can understand why God would say no. I am a doer and a self-motivated individual by nature. Therefore, after God rescued me from all my illnesses if He had left me with nothing to remind me where I come from, I know that I would easily become my own god and leave the throne of Christ.

You may wonder why I think this way. My answer to you is this: God has freed me from constant torment from Satan, where I was experiencing worse sickness than the physical pain I currently struggle with. Therefore, just as Jesus rescued me from that sickness that no doctors could explain to me growing up, I know He can remove my physical pain if that decision would be beneficial to my salvation. *There is a prayer I often pray to God*: "Lord, give me enough to take care of my family, to help those who are in need, and help Your Kingdom to advance. Do not give me more or less. Lord Jesus, do not take away anything in my life or give me anything that will hinder my walk with You." I started praying this prayer after I studied why King David prayed to God not to take his spirit from him (Psalm 51:11–12) after the prophet Nathan had confronted him about his sins. David remembered what became of King Saul when God left him and allowed an evil spirit to torment him (1 Samuel 16:14–23; 18:10; 19:9).

Praising God through chronic pain is not easy. It is a daily decision, choosing to listen to God's promises instead of the adversary's voice telling me I am defeated. In fact, unless I tell people about my pain or my daily struggle, they often don't know. On the contrary, when I tell people I am in pain, they often say, "You don't look like you are in pain."

I remember one of my coworkers suggested that I see her rheumatologist to explore recommendations to help with my pain. This particular visit was ordained by God; although she did not find a cure or a medicine that would help my pain, she spoke life to me as if it were God speaking. I remember after she reviewed the records and listened to what my concerns and struggles were as I fought with physical pain, she described my body *"as a beautiful house where everything on the outside seems okay, well-kept, and possibly without any visible blemish. However, inside there is a fire that cannot be seen, and the only way to calm it down is to make changes from the outside that impact the internal fire."* She further stated that acknowledging and accepting you have limitations and learning to say no, to stop and to rest is the most effective medicine for your chronic pain. She ended her statement by responding to my explanation that people see me as a healthy young woman and sometimes don't believe that I am not well. She said, "Those people are not your friends. Find new friends who will listen to you instead of judging you based on what they see." That doctor's visit changed my perspective about how to fight this chronic pain. I remember crying all the way home from the appointment because the doctor spoke to my soul, and I knew she was right.

Apostle Paul and Jesus are both prime examples of what it means to

> Rejoice always, pray continually, give thanks in
> all circumstances; for this is God's will for you in
> Christ Jesus. (1 Thessalonians 5:16–18)

The Scriptures do not say rejoice only when things are going well or when it appears that God has given you victories. My vow in my Christian walk is to do God's will, and Paul challenged me that it is God's will that I rejoice even when I am hurting. Yes, many times I pray and ask God to please take my soul from this decaying body when I feel like I cannot go another hour, minute, second, and day with the pain. Jesus reminds me in this world I will have trials/tribulations but to take heart because Jesus has overcome the world (John 16:33–34), which gives me hope that I will also overcome (1 John 5:4–5). When Satan tries to spew lies in my mind about God's love and sovereignty, I often study the book of Job to remind me who my enemy is. When Satan attempted to use Job's wife to turn his mind and heart from God's sovereignty, I love Job's response to his wife: His wife said to him,

> "Are you still trying to maintain your integrity? Curse God and die." But Job replied, "You talk like a foolish woman. Should we accept only good things from the hand of God and never anything bad?" So in all this, Job said nothing wrong. (Job 2:9–10)

People often ask how you maintain your joyful attitude when you experience some level of pain daily. My answer is God! Choosing to believe God's promises to be true.

> God will take away all their tears. There will be no more death or sorrow or crying or pain. All the old things have passed away. (Revelation 21:4 NLT)

When I read this scripture or listen to it being read by others, my soul leaps for joy knowing there is an end to the horror that I face in this world, which is not my final home. As I mentioned earlier, there are days when my faith, trusting in God's promises and protection, is under attack by Satan. During those moments, I often wanted to be alone and began to experience symptoms of depression such as lack of interest, crying, wishing God would take me home, mood swings, and often being short-tempered. Therefore, I am not saying living with chronic pain as a Christian is easy, but one thing I do know, if it were not for Jesus and His Spirit living in me, I would not make it.

In the seasons of my physical struggle, I must make a conscious decision to pray and hold on to God's Word. As a result, I seldom experience spiritual meltdowns. I remember a doctor once suggested that I join an online support group to help me cope with my symptoms by listening to/reading other people's experiences. After an hour of reading some of the stories and comments from others who suffer from chronic pain/diseases similar to my struggle, I became so depressed. At the time, many of them were young like me, in their twenties, successful in their careers and/or in college when their pain started. They all shared how chronic pain robbed them of their dreams, self-worth, and identity. Most of them were addicted to painkillers, unable to work, and were diagnosed with severe depression. I recalled one story about a young successful lawyer who experienced her first muscle cramp while working in her office and she could not move. Her story ended with a statement highlighting that was the day her dreams and life changed for the worse. I recalled saying to myself, these people's stories will not be mine. That was the last time I ever joined or read that support group blog. Instead, I decided to go back to God, my healer, my high priest, and plead my case before Him who is able to heal me or show me how to live with chronic pain. In Hebrews 4:15, we learn that our Lord Jesus Christ can empathize with our weaknesses. I have accepted that there are times when God will not take our pain or life stressors away, but He promises at the proper time He will restore us.

> And the God of all grace, who called you to his eternal glory in Christ, after you have suffered a little while, will himself restore you and make you strong, firm and steadfast. (1 Peter 5:10 NLT)

> Praise be to the God and Father of our Lord Jesus Christ! In his great mercy he has given us new birth into a living hope through the resurrection of Jesus Christ from the dead, and into an inheritance that can never perish, spoil, or fade. This inheritance is kept in heaven for you, who through faith are shielded by God's power until the coming of the salvation that is ready to be revealed in the last time. In all this you greatly rejoice, though now for a little while you may have had to suffer grief in all kinds of trials. These have come so that the proven genuineness

> of your faith—of greater worth than gold, which perishes even though refined by fire—may result in praise, glory and honor when Jesus Christ is revealed. Though you have not seen him, you love him; and even though you do not see him now, you believe in him and are filled with an inexpressible and glorious joy, for you are receiving the end result of your faith, the salvation of your souls. (1 Peter 1:3–10 NLT)

Learning to live with chronic pain and believing that God is able to heal me has never been a doubt in my mind because He had done it in my life before. My dilemma has always been knowing that God is able but not knowing if He is willing. I recall God leading me to read a profound scripture that changed my prayer when I went before Him regarding chronic pain.

> What sorrow awaits those who argue with their Creator. Does a clay pot argue with its maker? Does the clay dispute with the one who shapes it, saying, "Stop, you're doing it wrong!" Does the pot exclaim, "How clumsy can you be?" How terrible it would be if a newborn baby said to its father, "Why was I born?" or if it said to its mother, "Why did you make me this way?" (Isaiah 45:9 NLT)

God has rescued me from so many physical trials in my life. For example, I struggled with fainting spells as a child where I would become unconscious. He delivered me from that when doctors were not able to find any medical root for my spells. I recall having episodes where I felt like I was fainting, my eyes twitching, unable to speak, but I was able to hear everything that people were saying. I saw a neurologist; he ran several tests to determine if what I was experiencing were seizures, the scan came back that my brain waves were normal/optimal. They tried medication, but my body had a major swelling reaction to the treatment. Again, God rescued me from this sickness.

There are many more spiritual curses that God has rescued me from. If you read my encounter with Jesus, you know my sicknesses were part of a spiritual warfare where Satan was trying to capture my soul from God's eternal plan for my life. Glory be to God! God prevailed just as He has always done from the beginning. I share some of my victories to help you understand why I do not dare to question God's sovereignty, mercy, grace, and power to deliver me from the physical pain that I experience.

Chronic pain started to manifest in my life after God set me free from the evil spirits that had been tormenting me for many years. Choosing to trust God during trials in our lives takes courage. In addition, accepting and believing God knows best and His thoughts and decisions are for our benefit.

> "My thoughts are nothing like your thoughts," says the Lord. "And my ways are far beyond anything you could imagine." (Isaiah 55:8 NLT)

I believe deep in my soul if God knew removing this thorn from my flesh was beneficial, He would have done so just as He did in the past. The Bible says that everything happening in my life was written before I was born (Psalm 139); therefore, I am choosing to trust that He cares for me. Do you believe that Jesus loves you and is working everything out for you because He loves you? (Romans 8:28). Apostle Paul reminded the Disciples in Philippians 4:19,

> And my God will meet all your needs according to the riches of his glory in Christ Jesus.

During His ministry, Jesus reminded us about the goodness of our God as He taught His Disciples not to worry (Matthew 6:25–27). Are you living a defeated life, or is your life an example of faith despite your trials? My goal is when people look at me, I want Jesus's name to be glorified. What would your non-Christian friends and family say about you as a Christian when facing pain or trials of many kinds? Most importantly, how would your fellow Christians describe you as you face trials of many kinds?

Second Corinthians 5:1–10 (NLT) will continue to be the foundational hope and truth in my fight with chronic pain as a daughter of the living God until He heals me, calls me home, or comes to get me. Either one of these outcomes that I mentioned is a win for me. Apostle Paul reminded me and everyone who says Jesus is Lord,

> Our body is like a house we live in here on earth. When it is destroyed, we know that God has another body for us in Heaven. The new one will not be made by human hands as a house is made. This body will last forever. Right now we cry inside ourselves because we wish we could have our new body which we will have in Heaven. We will not be without a body. We will live in a new body. While we are in this body, we cry inside ourselves because things are hard for us. It is not that we want to die. Instead, we want to live in our new bodies. We want this dying body to be changed into a living body that lasts forever. It is God Who has made us ready for this change. He has given us His Spirit to show us what He has for us. We are sure of this. We know that while we are at home in this body we are not with the Lord. Our life is lived by faith. We do not live by what we see in front of us. We are sure we will be glad to be free of these bodies. It will be good to be at home with the Lord. So if we stay here on earth or go home to Him, we always want to please Him. For all of us must stand before Christ when He says who is guilty or not guilty. Each one will receive pay for what he has done. He will be paid for the good or the bad done while he lived in this body.

Meditating through this passage has given me significant confidence and joy in knowing that although I hurt physically while my spirit and soul live in this body on this earth, I am promised by Jesus, who was God in the flesh, that as long as I remain faithful until the end, my pain will be no more (Revelation 21:4). The reality is everyone's experience with pain will never be the same; therefore, everyone's coping mechanism will manifest differently. Prayerfully, as Christians/Disciples of Jesus Christ, our coping mechanism during a painful trial, whether physical or emotional, should be rooted in the promises of God's Words and actions through Jesus, who can sympathize with all our weaknesses (Hebrews 4:15–16; Hebrews 5:7). My daily personal goal as I strive to remain faithful through my physical pain is to enter God's rest that He promised until God mercifully grants me a new body.

> For anyone who enters God's rest has also rested from his own work, as God did from his. Therefore, let us do our best to enter that rest; so that no one will fall short because of the same kind of disobedience (Hebrews 4:10–11 CJB).

Let's enter God's rest with confidence, knowing this is all temporary as we use our gifts, victories, and trials to share His Word, patiently waiting for our day of deliverance from this decaying body.

CHAPTER 8

Unmerited Grace and Love

God is Love. Whoever lives in love lives in God,
and God in them. (1 John 4:16)

THE SPIRIT PROMPTED me to read Luke 6:27–36 and would not let me keep my thoughts to myself, even though I tried to. As always, the Counselor from the living God who lives inside of me won!

Our society uses the word *love* a lot. I would even argue that the word love is used across different religious groups and among atheists without them realizing they are speaking of God. The world's number one enemy since the Garden of Eden knew that love is a powerful tool when it is used as intended. Therefore, as he impersonates himself as a god throughout history, he manipulates the word love to be used in ways that hurt God (Revelation 13:6–8). What is the greatest commandment in God's law? In Deuteronomy 6:4–5 and 10:12, God reminded His chosen people that "God is one" and they must love Him with all their heart and with all their soul and with all their strength. The verse in Deuteronomy 10:12 further reminded us to fear God and to love Him. Jesus, the Word of God in flesh, relayed the same message to all His Disciples/Christians in Matthew 22:37–38:

"Teacher, which commandment is the greatest in
the Law?" Jesus declared, "Love the Lord your

God with all your heart and with all your soul
and with all your mind." This is the first and
greatest commandment.

Jesus did not just tell us that God is love; He went further by becoming the ultimate gift of love by dying on the cross without any guarantee that we would choose God (John 3:16–19, 1 Peter 2:21–24, Ephesians 3:14–21, John 13:34–35).

The word *grace* in Christian theology is defined as "the spontaneous, unmerited gift of the divine, favor in the salvation of sinners and the divine influence operating in individuals for their regeneration and sanctification" (*Britannica Dictionary*). According to this definition, grace is not something we earn; it is given to us. Think of what you and I were before we became a Christian and think of what you continue to struggle with today. If I had to earn God's grace, I know hell would be the automatic destination for me because I can never earn it, no matter how hard I might try. It is a gift!

> For by grace you have been saved through faith
> and this is not your own doing; it is the gift of
> God—not by works, so that no one can boast.
> For we are God's handiwork created in Christ
> Jesus to do good works which God prepared in
> advance for us to do. (Ephesians 2:8–10 NIV)

If you are reading this devotion and you have not decided to make Jesus the Lord of your life, the gift of God's grace is available to you as well. All you must do is accept it, open it, and use it. No matter where you are in your life, what others have said about you, or what you have experienced in your life, Jesus is ready to welcome you just as you are. He can transform you to become the beautiful butterfly you were intended to be from the day you were created.

Oftentimes, when we speak of love as a Disciple/Christian, we reference 1 Corinthians 13:4–8, and rightly so because this is the description and example of God throughout the entire Bible. The problem is we often use the passage but do not often apply it in our lives. Or we apply it to a degree/extent where there is a clause. You know what type of clauses I am referring to if we are honest with ourselves! For example, we make statements like, "God knows that I have been patient with… I have reached my limit." Or we say, "It is mine. I work hard for it. Why should I let someone else use it or give it to people who did not work for it or who are lazy?" The truth is the list can go on and on and on… Contrast our daily attitude toward ourselves and other people around us, reflect for a moment, and ask yourself if Jesus were to treat you or me the way you view or perceive yourself and others, where would you be today?

The Apostle Paul did not just understand the magnitude of God's love in his life; he experienced it, and out of gratitude for the grace, which is a gift from God through the Holy Spirit, he was able to write what love is and what love is not according to the overwhelming grace that God, through Jesus Christ, had shown him (Romans 7). If you have not taken the time to study Apostle Paul, do it! In my opinion, after Jesus, Paul is the second example we should imitate as we strive to be like Jesus. He mirrors Jesus's mission in human form. One of the amazing characteristics of Apostle Paul that is worth imitating is his humility about not taking any credit for his worldly or spiritual accomplishments. Instead, he chose to boast in Jesus, our Savior and Lord (2 Corinthians 11:16, 12:6–10). You might be wondering when I will share about Luke 6. How can I begin to understand or embrace Jesus's teaching in Luke 6:17–36 if I do not spend some time understanding His unmerited grace and love for me?

CHAPTER 9

Love Beyond Measure

JESUS MADE MANY practical points that we can learn from in verses 17–36 of Luke 6. My focus will mostly be on verses 27–36, which prompted me to write this devotional. Prior to Jesus's lesson on how we should treat our enemy, I was not surprised by His example of grace that He allowed to be given to so many people. In verses 17–19, the Scriptures state that the people came to hear Him and to be healed. Take a moment to process what is happening in these passages that we so often miss as Disciples, teachers, and preachers of Jesus Christ. The Scripture does not say the people came to join His ministry, nor did it say that since they were not part of Jesus's ministry, He limited His healing gift. Jesus, in the flesh, was a man of community, and He welcomed everyone, even the ones who rejected Him. The passage said He healed them all. The second observation was in verses 20–26, where Jesus turned to His Disciples, highlighting areas of their lives that are or will be a stumbling block in their Discipleship journey, and gave them a heavenly vision. My third observation: Jesus further spoke to the heart of the wealthy who rely on their earthly comfort instead of the everlasting comfort that God promises those who endure until the end.

In verses 27–31,

> He turned his attention to anyone listening and challenged them by saying, "Love your enemies, do good to those who hate you, bless those who curse you and pray for those who mistreat you. If someone slaps you on one cheek, turn to them the other also. If someone takes your coat, do not withhold your shirt from them. Give to everyone who ask you, and if anyone takes what belongs to you, do not demand it back. Do to others as you would have them do to you."

Take a moment to read these Scriptures a few times and meditate on them. Jesus is not asking you and me to practice something that He Himself has not endured. Read the crucifixion account in both the book of Luke, chapters 22–24, and Matthew, chapters 26–28. In the '90s, WWJD ("What would Jesus do?") was a very popular slogan. However, as I continue to grow in my walk with Jesus, I believe WDJD ("What did Jesus do?") is a more appropriate slogan for Christians because Jesus has left us examples of how to manage everything (2 Timothy 3:16, John 14:25–27). Our attempt to minimize or translate what Jesus said to what makes us feel comfortable is not loving Jesus, and the Spirit of truth does not live in us (1 John 3:24, 4:6).

Honestly, I have heard and read different statements made about the passage in Luke 6:27–32. We often try to translate what we think Jesus meant to say so that we can escape the clear instructions that He gives us because we cannot bear it. I am nowhere near perfecting any of these commands/challenges/instructions by Jesus, and I do not think I will ever be. However, what I will not do is act foolishly by convincing myself that Jesus does not really mean if someone hates me that I must love them, or if they mistreat me, I must pray for them. If they slap me on one cheek, turn the other, and so on. What I am choosing to do is pray, asking God to help me to be obedient if/when I face these circumstances in my journey with Jesus. The fact is, Jesus demonstrated for us in different passages throughout His ministry that He meant every Word that He spoke. Jesus is God and clearly stated, "My words are spirit and life" (John 6:63).

If we want to stay engrafted with Him, we must obey Him (John 15). Studying the crucifixion is one of my favorite Bible studies, starting with Jesus washing the feet of Judas, who would later betray Him, to Peter denying Him as He had predicted, to Jesus crying, "Father, forgive them, for they know not what they do," while they were killing Him. Then being separated from God because He took my sins, forgiving the sinful man at the cross, and the resurrection to eternal life that He promises to those who stay faithful (Matthew 26, 27, 28; Luke 23).

Jesus did not stop at verse 31; He continued to challenge men to reflect the heart of God.

> If you love those who love you, what credit is that to you? Even sinners love those who love them. And if you do good to those who are good to you, what credit is that to you? Even sinners do that. And if you lend to those from whom you expect repayment, what credit is that to you? Even sinners lend to sinners, expecting to be repaid in full. But love your enemies, do good to them, and lend to them without expecting to get anything back. Then your reward will be great, and you will be children of the Most High, because he is kind to the ungrateful and wicked. Be merciful, just as your Father is merciful. (Luke 6:32–36)

As I meditate on these commands of Jesus, I envision Him restoring God's love that Satan has distorted and planted in mankind's mind and heart. Satan's love is conditional: you love me, I will love you back; you serve me, I will serve you; you forgive me, then I will forgive you, etc. God's love for you and me is always steady. Our mistakes, emotional turmoil, *our goodness*, and our sins against Him do not change His love for us. I love this particular verse that is part of a Christian song, "Jesus loves me when I am bad, but it makes Him very sad." Although as a mental health worker, I do not like the wording "when I am bad," I love the concept of it. When we make bad choices or decisions, it hurts God, but He still loves us and is waiting for us to return home to His love (Luke 15:11–32).

I believe there is goodness in every human being—yes, even the worst person you can think of, because Scripture says God "… set eternity in the human heart" (Ecclesiastes 3:10–11). God, in His infinite love, calls us as His followers to love beyond measure like He does for you and me. Jesus challenges us not just to say that we love our enemy but to demonstrate our love for them through actions. Jesus, in human flesh, lived in this world for thirty-three years and probably saw and heard it all. Consequently, His instructions to those who claim to walk with God were specific, so specific that at the end of verse 35, He reminded us why His commands are an expectation if we claim to be His followers. Jesus states we must be different from the way the world treats *their enemy because* God "is kind to the ungrateful and wicked."

> Be merciful, just as your Father is merciful. (Luke 6:36)

Who are the ungrateful and wicked? I am, we are. We deserve eternal condemnation, but instead, He took our sins upon Himself so that I/we might choose Him (1 Peter 3:17–22, 2 Corinthians 5:17–21).

As I reflect on my own struggle with the area of loving others, I have learned that it is easier for me to love my enemy to the extent that I have experienced in my walk with God thus far. The area that I am continuing to grow in is love for my fellow Disciples/Christians who profess to be followers of Jesus but who continue making choices that are contrary to what the Word of God teaches.

My difficulty lies in my own pride that they should know better because they have vowed that Jesus is Lord on the day of baptism. However, over the years, I continue to strive, holding true to 1 John

4:7–8, 19–20, and 1 John 3:10, which have helped me fight against my sinful nature, which is not in agreement with God's grace and mercy. The Spirit of God once convicted me that He does not need my help because He can handle His children: "Annaika, you focus on being obedient to My Word" (Matthew 6:15; Colossians 3:13). In closing, take some time to reflect on the boundaries of your love for yourself, family, friends, fellow Christians, and neighbors/everyone, and see if it matches God's love or Satan's version of love. Specifically, the people whom you feel have done wrong against you or a cause that you are passionate about. Let us fight to love without any condition just as God has shown us mercy and love beyond measure.

The Jar of Salvation

> Then he said to the crowd, "If any of you wants
> to be my follower, you must give up your own
> way, take up your cross daily, and follow me."
> (Luke 9:23 NLT)

MY HUSBAND OFTEN tells this screensaver story when he speaks about Satan's spirit of delusion that often attracts us into his domain. The story goes that a man was given two doors to choose from. When the man opens the first door, he sees laughter, happiness, success, fun, and entertainment. As he opens the second door, all he sees is a peaceful calm space with the sound of wind and soft songs. The man automatically assumed the first door must be the better choice because it seemed so alive and fun. To his surprise, as he entered the first door, he learned that it was a screensaver! Behind that delusion is heartache, pain, disappointment, rejection, and death. The door with the screensaver that appeared to be boring and uninteresting was the one he was truly seeking. That door had joy, laughter, peace, enjoyment, and everlasting reward and contentment. I reference this story to highlight that Jesus's teaching for many people might sound overbearing and even burdensome when it is read (Luke 14:26, Luke 14:33). Nevertheless, when a person takes the time to get to know

Jesus and His mission to seek and save their soul, His message is the opposite of what our adversary (Satan) wants us to believe.

There are several stories in the Bible where the Spirit of delusion manifested in people's lives. These delusional spirits make people seek earthly things to fill the different voids that they have. Many people are familiar with the rich young ruler story referenced in Mark 10:17–27, where he allows the love of his wealth to hinder his opportunity to be with God for eternity. Like the rich young ruler, although we know or have been warned that we are heading in the wrong direction, we are stuck. Our earthly comfort blinds us to the eternal danger that we are walking or running toward. For this young man, it was his wealth that was the obstacle that prevented him from answering Jesus's call. However, for many of us, it's simple things like ungratefulness, a romantic relationship, thirst for power, fear, guilt, shame, greed, people-pleasing, and/or other empty desires we often choose over Jesus's calling.

Satan makes us believe that these earthly desires are necessary to make us feel whole or complete. For example, there has been an increase in suicide incidents among famous rich people. Why would rich people kill themselves when they have so much wealth? The answer is simple: there is no earthly wealth or possession that can bind or fill voids that people are longing for to heal their heart/soul (Ecclesiastes 2:1–11). Only God—through Jesus Christ—can bind and heal the hearts of men (Psalm 147:3).

> And I heard a loud voice from the throne saying, "Look! God's dwelling place is now among the people, and he will dwell with them. They will be his people, and God himself will be with them and be their God. 'He will wipe every tear from their eyes. There will be no more death or mourning or crying or pain, for the old order of things has passed away.'" (Revelation 21:3–4 NIV)

There is a woman who I believe encountered a similar dilemma in her life in John 4:1–26. We do not know why Jesus encountered the woman at the time that He did; however, we know that God is always intentional with every decision that He makes. Could it be possible that the Samaritan woman was crying out to God about her life struggles? Or could it be that God saw her desire to change but she felt stuck? Can we relate to these feelings?

A woman's journey: the woman at the well

> Now Jesus learned that the Pharisees had heard that he was gaining and baptizing more Disciples than John—although in fact it was not Jesus who baptized, but his Disciples. So he left Judea and went back once more to Galilee. (John 4:1–26 NIV)

The Scriptures simply say that Jesus left an area where His ministry was thriving to go to Galilee once more. Galilee is Jesus's hometown, which He had referenced as not being able to perform miracles due to their *lack of faith* (Mark 6:4–6). God instructed Jesus to go, and He obeyed and went. I know the attitude of my heart would have been, "God, why these people? I went to them already, and they rejected You." As we can see, that is not Jesus's heart because He trusted His Father. Is this our attitude when God calls us to do things that don't align with our understanding or do not make sense to our logical minds? There are different theories about why Jesus had to go through Samaria instead of all the different routes He could have traveled. However, I believe God knew there were souls in Samaria who needed His everlasting love.

> Now he had to go through Samaria. So he came to a town in Samaria called Sychar, near the plot of ground Jacob had given to his son Joseph. Jacob's well was there, and Jesus, tired as he was

from the journey, sat down by the well. It was
about noon. (Verses 4–6)

God is always precise in His overall plan. The fact that the
woman came to get water at noon, which is known as the hottest
time of day in the area when other people from the town would not
likely come to draw water, tells me the woman was isolated and was
protecting herself from her community. It is very possible that God
saw this woman's physical and internal struggles and sent Jesus on a
mission to rescue her (Luke 5:31–32).

As you reflect on the Samaritan's decision, think of your life.
What are the sins in your life that are preventing you from con-
necting with God? Who or what are you hiding from in your life
where you feel alone, helpless, and invisible? You see, God knew this
woman needed deliverance, and He knows that you do as well. To
God, you are visible, and you matter. The Samaritan woman came to
draw earthly water and instead found eternal water.

> When a Samaritan woman came to draw water,
> Jesus said to her, 'Will you give me a drink?' (His
> Disciples had gone into the town to buy food.)
> The Samaritan woman said to him, 'You are a
> Jew, and I am a Samaritan woman. How can you
> ask me for a drink?' (For Jews do not associate
> with Samaritans—verses 5–9)

The Samaritan woman saw the heart of God before even knowing she was speaking with God in the flesh, by recognizing that this
Jew went against the norm of the society at the time. I honestly
believe Jesus, the Son of God, could have satisfied His thirst without
the woman's water, but neither the water nor the thirst was His mission. His mission was to win the heart and soul of the woman. How
often do we miss the mission of God because we focus on the physical matters of this world instead of the spiritual lessons or blessings
that God has for us?

> Jesus answered her, "If you knew the gift of God
> and who it is that asks you for a drink, you would
> have asked him and he would have given you liv-
> ing water." (verse 10)

I see this exchange as the grace and merciful Gospel of Jesus Christ. Jesus knew this woman was seeking something more than the water she came to draw, so He introduced God's mercy and everlasting gift to her, which was eternal life/salvation.

> "Sir," the woman said, "you have nothing to draw
> with, and the well is deep. Where can you get
> this living water? Are you greater than our father
> Jacob, who gave us the well and drank from it
> himself, as did also his sons and his livestock."
> (verses 11–12)

The woman's response to Jesus made it clear that her focus is on the physical, religious, and political matters of her world. The Samaritan woman's facts were correct, but I love how Jesus did not let historical facts or earthly truth interfere with His spiritual mission. Frequently, as Christians/Disciples of Jesus Christ, we allow the facts of our culture or environment to influence our reaction instead of focusing on the mission.

> Jesus answered, "Everyone who drinks this water
> will be thirsty again, but whoever drinks the
> water I give them will never thirst. Indeed, the
> water I give them will become in them a spring of
> water welling up to eternal life." (verses 13–14)

Jesus did not entertain the woman's statements but, in contrast, drew her back to His mission of introducing her to eternal life. In fact, her question to Jesus about being greater than Jacob is true, and Jesus, in His ego, could have challenged the woman but instead stayed steadfast in His effort to win her over for God. There is so much we can learn from Jesus's interaction with the woman, as God's ambassador to a world that is always ready for a fight to justify their points. If we, as followers of Jesus, imitate His focus on humility and salvation, we would help so many people to draw closer to God.

> The woman said to him, "Sir, give me this water so that I won't get thirsty and have to keep coming here to draw water." (verse 15)

The woman was still missing the spiritual gift that Jesus was offering to her. Her focus is on meeting her physical needs, which is temporary. The woman's response should resonate with each of us because we tend to get impatient with God because we want immediate gratification. However, God is patient with us just as Jesus demonstrated with the woman, guiding us to see the long-term effects or benefits. It's obvious by the woman's response she is seeking something long term and consistent in her life. The woman must have thought, *Wow! Water that can prevent me from coming to this well, which will stop me from living in fear, isolation, shame, and rejection from others? Give it to me!* In fact, she was right because Jesus did empty her earthly jar and filled her jar with spiritual drinks to free her from Satan's bondage.

> He told her, "Go, call your husband and come back." "I have no husband," she replied. Jesus said to her, "You are right when you say you have no husband. The fact is, you have had five husbands, and the man you now have is not your husband. What you have just said is quite true." (verses 16–18)

This part of the interaction I call the repentance and transformation Gospel of Jesus as He invited the woman to face her life of sins. He waited for the perfect opportunity to join the woman in her earthly mindset, which forced her to look at her life. Jesus's action communicated to the woman, "I am not concerned about the law or political arguments of this world, but I am concerned about your soul and salvation."

> "Sir," the woman said, "I can see that you are a prophet. Our ancestors worshiped on this mountain, but you Jews claim that the place where we must worship is in Jerusalem." (verses 19–20)

Despite Jesus's effort to bring the woman to spiritual thinking, she continued to focus on the tangible and facts of the earth. How often do we do the exact thing to God in our search for Him or walk with Him?

> "Woman," Jesus replied, "believe me, a time is coming when you will worship the Father neither on this mountain nor in Jerusalem. You Samaritans worship what you do not know; we worship what we do know, for salvation is from the Jews. Yet a time is coming and has now come when the true worshipers will worship the Father in the Spirit and in truth, for they are the kind of worshipers the Father seeks. God is spirit, and his worshipers must worship in the Spirit and in truth." (verses 21–24)

Jesus realized that unless He addressed the woman's questions and fixation on the earthly laws or facts, she would not see the spiritual gift that He was offering her. Therefore, Jesus addressed her concerns and added the spiritual facts about true worship according to God's plan.

> The woman said, "I know that Messiah" (called Christ) "is coming. When he comes, he will explain everything to us." Then Jesus declared, "I, the one speaking to you—I am he." (verses 25–26)

Did you notice how after Jesus addressed her fixations and incorporated spiritual facts in His answers, the Samaritan woman, in turn, responded with a spiritual mindset? And she was able to receive the gift of God.

Reflection

As I reflected on the story of the Samaritan woman, I realized that I have been where she was at various times in my life. Have you ever felt so empty in your life that you are seeking to fill that void? Wishing for answers and the answers that you are seeking seem so unreachable or impossible? Oftentimes, things that we attempt to fill our jar with only last for a little while or cause us more pain. We often try to fill the void with tangible things such as relationships, pleasures, success/accomplishments, education, people-pleasing, and drugs/alcohol. Unfortunately, many people feel so defeated by the void of hopelessness from the empty feelings of life that they are just existing instead of living.

Are you willing to leave your worldly jar at the foot of the cross and let God fill your jar with everlasting life? Jesus offered the woman an everlasting solution to fill the voids in her life which is also available to all of us today. After Jesus brought the Samaritan woman to a spiritual state of mind and declared, "I, the one speaking to you—I am He" (John 4:26), the Holy Spirit has led me to think deeper and see the metaphor of her action. In John 4:28–29, the Scripture says,

> Then leaving her water jar, the woman went back
> to the town and said to the people, "Come, see
> a man who told me everything I ever did. Could
> this be the Messiah?"

I see the woman leaving the jar at the well with Jesus as a metaphoric sign of deliverance and transformation. I believe the woman did not only leave the jar, but she also left her feelings of fear, shame, isolation, hopelessness, and her sinful life.

How can I draw such a conclusion? The simple fact that she ran toward the town to share her newly found hope and deliverance, despite what they might have thought of her, conveyed she is free. Her radical boldness drew the town's curiosity. They came to see Jesus for themselves. Reflecting on your own life, what areas in your inner soul/heart do you need Jesus to fill with "everlasting water?" Jesus is calling us to leave whatever our "jar" might be at the foot of the cross.

Another lesson we can learn from studying this message, Jesus expects transformation when He calls people to join His kingdom (John 4:15–16). Jesus offers the Samaritan woman salvation, and after she says, "Give it to me, Jesus," He addressed the sins in her life that was hindering her spiritual fulfillment. What is holding you back from saying yes to Jesus's call or giving yourself fully to His mission?

Most individuals want the gift of salvation without the willingness to change by continuing to live their lives against God's commands. Scripture warns us that unless we transform from living by the flesh to living through the Spirit of God, we will not enter God's kingdom (Galatians 5:13–26; Revelation 2:4–5). We learned that Jesus's act of love through His patience, kindness, and willingness to speak the truth in humility to the woman is what led to people believing in God. Our willingness to allow Jesus through the Holy Spirit to transform our lives can be the tool that God uses to free us from our lives of bondage and save many people from Satan's delusions.

Studying Jesus's encounter with the Samaritan woman has several life lessons that we can apply in our walk with Jesus. For example, Jesus gave the Apostles a glimpse of what His kingdom will be like when they found Him speaking with the Samaritan woman. John 4:27 says they were *surprised* to have found Him speaking with a woman, not just a woman but one from a different culture, yet nobody questioned Jesus. We should all have the desire to be like Jesus by obeying God when He sends us. We should also desire to learn how to filter through the noises that Satan uses to distract us when we are having conversations with people so that we do not drift away from God's mission. This lesson applies to when we speak to Christians and non-Christians. Jesus demonstrated His love in action as He patiently speaks to the woman with grace, truth, and love. In contrast, the Samaritan woman taught us what we might know as facts in this world are not God's facts in His kingdom. When we encounter Jesus, we must be willing to surrender everything that hinders our spiritual growth. Lastly, the courage, joy, and everlasting promise we receive from knowing Jesus is worth telling everyone we know despite potential societal risks.

CHAPTER 11

Are You a Pharisee?
Part 1

> Meanwhile, when many thousands of the crowd had gathered so that they were trampling on one another, Jesus began to speak first to his Disciples, "Be on your guard against the yeast of the Pharisees, which is hypocrisy. Nothing is hidden that will not be revealed, and nothing is secret that will not be made known. So then whatever you have said in the dark will be heard in the light, and what you have whispered in private rooms will be proclaimed from the housetops." (Luke 12:1–3 NLT)

AS I READ this direct instruction from Jesus in Luke 12:1, telling the Disciples to be on guard against "the yeast of the Pharisees," I started asking myself, "Am I a Pharisee?" Who were the Pharisees? In my Christian journey, I have heard many teachings about Pharisees and many warnings not to be like them. However, I never took the time to personally learn about them. How can we be on guard about someone or something that we don't take the time to study and build our own conviction? Jesus's warning about the yeast of the Pharisees tells me there are different types of yeast. He also sent a message to His followers warning them to be vigilant against the corruptible yeast, or in the same way the Pharisees were contaminated could also happen to them. I decided to read about the types and nature of yeast to have a much better understanding of Jesus's warning. Overall, I learned yeast is fast in production. Although asexuality is the primary way of reproduction, they can also produce sexually. After my short research, I concluded that yeast is not a bad organism; however, it can be harmful depending on how it is used or the type of infection that has developed or contracted into your body.

Learning about yeast helps me better understand why Jesus was very specific in His warning. Jesus went further to name the type of yeast, *hypocrisy*. As I try to connect what I read about yeast and Jesus's warning, I can't help but imagine the Pharisees' yeast is more connected to the infectious pathogenic yeast that can be harmful and sometimes deadly to the human body. Since bread is known to have been a part of the Israelite daily diet, I imagine Jesus looking at a loaf of bread when He made the statement, because the Disciples could easily connect His lesson to what they were familiar with.

Who were the Pharisees?

According to biblical historians, the Pharisees were highly regarded men from the Jewish religious party who were focused on reinforcing oral traditions that were man-made, known as the "unwritten Torah." At some point in history (200 CE), the Jews decided to incorporate the teachings of the Pharisees into Jewish Law. The Sadducees, who were the Torah keepers (first five books of the Hebrew scriptures), were against the Pharisees' concept of interpreting the Torah to apply it to everyday situations. The Sadducees believed the Torah should be applied as it is written; no interpretation should be applied. The Pharisees were not a political party but a group of scholars and pietists. Their responsibility was to apply the Torah Law through interpretation according to the circumstances that were presented. Some Pharisees also served as scribes during the first century, where they had knowledge of the law and drafted legal documents. The Pharisees' intention was to encourage people not to "blindly follow the letter of the law even if it conflicted with reason or conscience." The goal of the Pharisees was to harmonize the teachings of the Torah with life-relevant practices that people could easily follow (Jewish History: *Encyclopedia Britannica*).

What was the life of a Pharisee like? How did the Pharisees display the act of hypocrisy in their lives?

Reading about who the Pharisees were and their role in the spiritual community, it is no surprise to me that Satan utilized them to go against the principle of God's law. Going back to the yeast warning, I can easily see how their yeast became toxic to their spiritual journey and easily influenced those who listened and followed them. I can also see how their intentions may have started as God's purpose to provide clarity, then they drifted away by becoming their own god. Instead of God being the center of life, they became the god of their society. Therefore, it is also no surprise to me that they rejected Jesus's teaching. Jesus declared Himself to be the only accurate and true interpreter of the Law according to God's will.

Jesus, in many of His teachings, stated that He was God and He speaks on behalf of God (John 12:49, John 8:38; John 14:10; John 17:25). In Matthew chapter 23, Jesus challenged the Pharisees' hypocrisy, but He did not say that everything they told the people was wrong. On the contrary, Jesus encouraged the crowd and His Disciples to do what the Pharisees told them but not do what they do. It seems to me the root of their hypocrisy was that they were not doers of their own teaching. In my observation, since they sat on the throne of leadership (Matthew 23:2), they perceived themselves as above the law; therefore, they did not feel that the law of God fully applied to them.

In Matthew 28:18–20, Jesus calls everyone who professes to be His Disciples to become teachers of His commands, which is what the Pharisees were known to be. Have you ever considered yourself a Pharisee? I know if we are honest with ourselves as we read this question, the answer is no. On the contrary, as I dive into this devotional,

I have a different perspective about Pharisees. Jesus calls us to apply a different yeast in our lives as His Disciples. Jesus called you and me to be engaged in the mission as He Himself modeled for us during His earthly ministry. The Pharisees loved being in the position of a commander or a king but not a soldier. Because as a soldier, you are required to engage in the fight, which they were not willing to do.

As we are learning and teaching the Bible, we can easily teach the written law or scriptures but not the Gospel according to Jesus. The Pharisees focused on the law instead of the heart of God. Everyone who professes that Jesus's standard is our way of life can easily become a Pharisee. As I study Jesus's ministry, I am learning how I subconsciously sway to the Pharisee's frame of mind when my intention is to allow the Word to transform my life. So then, I can show grace and truth through Jesus Christ to everyone whom God allows me to minister to. According to John 1:14, when the

> Word became a human being (Jesus) and lived with us, and we saw his Sh'khinah (Divine presence) the Sh'khinah, of the Father's only son full of grace and truth. (CJB)

Does your Christian walk reflect God's divine presence living in us where we show grace and do not compromise the truth of God? In Matthew 5:20, Jesus says,

> For I tell you unless your righteousness surpasses that of the Pharisees and the teachers of the law, you will certainly not enter the kingdom of heaven.

The Pharisees lived their lives as spectators for the praise of men instead of praise from God. They also enjoyed the physical wealth they acquired from using the law of God for their own benefit. What I have learned through this devotion is that the Pharisees did some things right, but they fell short by worshiping the law of God instead of God Himself. Three years ago, I started realizing a pattern throughout Jesus's ministry as I studied Him. He had a purpose for everything He did, and that purpose was to please His Father. I, in turn, started examining my heart and purpose in my walk with God, and it has been eye-opening. I have found myself saying yes and no to things for a different purpose, which is to glorify God, not people or my personal ego. Ask yourself, why do you do what you do? Is God's law a guide for your life, and is learning His heart your goal in your Christian walk?

CHAPTER 12

Are You a Pharisee? Part II

Be on your guard against the yeast of the Pharisees, which is hypocrisy. There is nothing concealed that will not be disclosed or hidden that will not be made known. What you have said in the dark will be heard in the daylight, and what you have whispered in the ear in the inner rooms will be proclaimed from the roofs. (Luke 12:1–3 NIV)

"Be careful," Jesus said to them. "Be on your guard against the yeast of the Pharisees and Sadducees." (Matthew 16:6 NIV)

ACCORDING TO THE *Merriam-Webster* dictionary, *hypocrisy* is defined as "a person who puts on a false appearance of virtue or religion," or "a person who acts in contradiction to his or her stated beliefs or feelings." The dictionary went further in describing *hypocrisy* as "a feigning to be what one is not or to believe what one does not: behavior that contradicts what one claims to believe or feel." The word *hypocrisy* that is used in the New Testament in the Greek language is *hypokrisis*, which simply means "acting on a stage" (*Hebrew-Greek Key Word Study Bible*).

Jesus tells us not to be actors in our mission as the keepers and teachers of the Word of God. The Word of God is meant to be alive and active and is meant to change lives (Hebrews 4:12–13). Our Lord Jesus, who became the Word in the flesh (John 1:14), dedicated His life while on this earth to show us how to rise above "the yeast of the Pharisees."

How can we supersede the Pharisees if we are not living a life that even resembles them? Yes, our goal is to be like Jesus! Jesus's goal throughout His ministry was to show God's heart in a society that was so divided by laws instead of truth. I believe there is a lot we can learn from the Pharisees. Lesson number one, are we a student of the Bible? Lesson number two, do we desire to teach or share the gospel with others? Lesson number three, are we passionate about the Word of God being applicable to every situation that we face in our lives? Unlike the Pharisees, we have a Rabbi/Teacher who lived His life as an example of what the law in action looks like. Jesus became the Word of God in human flesh (John 1:1–18) to demonstrate the Word in action.

The Pharisees had an opportunity to complete their spiritual journey with the Messiah in their presence, teaching them how to supersede their own doctrine. Instead of welcoming Jesus, they rejected Him and spent their energy working to trap Him into their own rules and laws (Matthew 19:3–9, Mark 8:11–12, Mark 12:13–17; there are many more examples). Therefore, they became slaves to the laws that were given by God to set them free. The same Law that was to set them free is the same law Satan used to blind them from the grace and truth of God through Jesus Christ. Consequently, although the Pharisees claimed to see God and understood God, they became blinded by their religious beliefs and hypocrisy (John 9:39–41 NIV).

Reflection

What does your walk with Jesus reflect? What areas in your life do you need to examine and change to help you lean toward the heart of God instead of worshiping His laws? I know we might be tempted, after reading this devotional, to point our fingers toward many religious leaders, family, or friends who claim to be servant of God and who might fit the description of a Pharisee according to your experience or observations. I would like to caution you not to spend your energy focusing on people's shortcomings in their walk with God. He promises everyone will give an account (Romans 14:10–12; Matthew 12:36) for their personal walk with Him.

God will not be mocked; each of us will reap what we sow (Galatians 6:7–10). My prayer and hope for us is to examine our personal walk with God! We all will stand before God for the choices that we make in our Christian walk. Our pastor, priest, clergy, elders, teachers, deacons, and ministry leaders are not responsible for your salvation; you are (Matthew 16:24–27). We each have our own cross to carry as we hope to hear this statement from Jesus, "Well done, my good and faithful servant" (Matthew 25:21). Yes, if called by God, the spiritual leaders in our lives are given a unique responsibility to help guide us toward Jesus, but they are not responsible for our decision to seek God with all our heart, might, and soul (Jeremiah 29:13). Don't let anyone or anything rob you of the opportunity to be one with God through Jesus Christ (John 15:1–17). Let's strive to rise above the yeast of the Pharisees and encourage others to do the same by our own life example, allowing the law/scriptures to transform our heart/soul to be like Jesus as His students/ Disciples.

Weekly Reflections
Prelude

Having Bible knowledge and understanding is great; however, if the scriptures are not living and active in our lives, it is all in vain (Hebrews 4:12–13). The weekly selections contain thought-provoking insights that will prayerfully transform us to be more like Jesus in our spiritual journey. James 1:23–27 challenges us to not just merely listen or read the scriptures; it says,

> But if you look carefully into the perfect law that sets you free, and if you do what it says and don't forget what you heard, then God will bless you for doing it.

My prayer and vision are for us to take these scriptures, meditate on them, and apply them to our lives every day, allowing the living Word of God to transform our minds. These short reflections have enabled me to draw closer to God, and I hope that they will assist you in your journey with God through our Lord Jesus Christ.

Week 1

> Do not be overcome by evil, but overcome evil with good. (Romans 12:21 NIV)

I was in line at Costco waiting to get gas when a person came from the other lane, cut me off, and took my spot. At that moment, many thoughts came through my mind. Believe me, my initial thoughts were not holy! I could hear the Spirit saying, "Recognize Satan when you see him manifesting before you! The person is not your enemy; Satan is." The different scriptures that rang through my ears were these: "Blessed are the meek, for they will inherit the earth" (Matthew 5:5), and "Blessed are the peacemakers, for they will be called children of God" (Matthew 5:9). What this gentleman did was evil, or we would say mean or inconsiderate. I would have been justified in defending my rights.

As a daughter of the living God with the guidance of the Holy Spirit, I chose to overcome what the devil intended for evil with good. This man may have walked away feeling good or maybe horrible, but I left Costco thanking God for His faithfulness. The driver who was behind me said, "How do you remain so cool?" And she stated, "I was mad for you!"

I said, "Ma'am, I can't take any credit. This is all God. I shared with her I had a good time with the Lord this morning that prepared me for many moments like this. Look for areas in your day where you can choose to defeat the evil scheme with good according to God's command!"

Week 2

> Because they regard not the work of the Lord,
> nor the operation of his hands, he shall destroy
> them, and not build them up. (Psalm 28:7 NIV)

What do you find yourself most concerned about? What areas in your life do you know you are not being obedient to God's work? Let's choose the work of the Lord and His perfect example through Jesus Christ in our lives so that He can build us up to our fullest potential. The best way to assess this area of your life is to observe where and what you spend most of your time doing, thinking about, or wishing for. Where your energy is being spent is usually a clear indication of your work.

Week 3

> Forgive our sins, as we also forgive everyone who
> sins against us. (Luke 11:4 TKJT)

Jesus, in His prayer while teaching His Disciples how to pray, added this statement. We all need forgiveness because we have all sinned against God (Romans 3:23). Reflect on your life today; whom in your life do you need to forgive? Your first reaction might be, "I have forgiven everyone who has wronged me in my life." If you are driven like me, I would suggest that you go through your list and examine your heart as you think of these people. If you experience that gut feeling as you think about anyone on your list, you have not forgiven. You may have distanced yourself, avoided the person, dismissed them, or moved away from them, but you may not have resolved it in your heart. Resolving in your heart simply means, as a child of God, you have given the person a clean slate, just as God has done for you. A clean slate does not mean the person's wrong against you is forgotten, but it's knowing that you and that person will stand before God to give an account for everything you have done (Romans 14:12). God is the final judge for all. And Jesus says in Matthew 6:15,

> But if you do not forgive others their sins, your heavenly father will not forgive you.

I once asked myself a question that I would like to leave with you: Is that person worth your soul being separated from God for eternity?

Week 4

> Be alert and of sober mind. Your enemy the devil prowls around like a roaring lion looking for someone to devour. (1 Peter 5:8 NIV)

Growing up around individuals in my life who were often drunk, when I initially read this scripture, I connected it to having a sober mind from alcohol. Although this interpretation might be true for some people, I learned the writer is speaking of a deeper pollution of the mind that comes in different forms. Think about where you are in life at this time. What has Satan filled your mind with that continues to distract you from God's purpose for your life?

Week 5

> The Lord is my shepherd; I lack nothing. (Psalm 23:1 NIV)

Who is the Lord of your life? The word *Lord* signifies that someone or something has full authority, power, and influence over your life. That person or thing is your master and is also the source of your being. Is that who Jesus is in your life? When David wrote this verse, it is obvious he was referring to how he views God's authority in his life. God gave David the confidence that he lacks nothing as long as his Creator is his shepherd. Does this message reflect your relationship with Jesus? Jesus calls us to carry our burdens to Him (Matthew 11:28–30), and Paul confidently reminds us that our God will provide for all our needs (Philippians 4:19). Who is your Lord and your Shepherd? To whom have you pledged your allegiance (Romans 6:17)? Oftentimes, there are many things or people who fill that role in our lives, such as career advancement, children, relationships, wealth, etc. You fill in the blank! Can you confidently say Jesus is your Lord, Shepherd, and Master of your life?

Week 6

> Here I am! I stand at the door and knock. If any-
> one hears my voice and opens the door, I will
> come in and eat with that person and they with
> me. (Revelation 3:20 NIV)

Jesus, in this Scripture, is speaking to the church in Laodicea. The people He was talking to were already claiming to be His Disciples. The church allowed sins to infiltrate their lives and changed their course away from God. Jesus, being the Chief Priest, is calling them to return to Him. When Jesus walked among His followers in John 14:6–7, He declared that He was the only way to God. In Revelation 3:21, He is reminding and persuading the church that His door is always open for them to come back if they choose to repent. He is calling the church back, hoping like the prodigal son, they will return home. What areas in your life do you need to hear God's voice? He is ready to take you back (Luke 15:11–32).

Week 7

> And when the Chief Shepherd appears, you will
> receive the crown of glory that will never fade
> away. (1 Peter 5:4 NIV)

We are all running a race in a world that has fallen people! There is a spiritual war against our soul, the flesh (sinful nature) versus the Spirit of God (holiness) (Galatians 5:16–18). Both the flesh and the Spirit have a destination at the end of this battle (Romans 8:6). In whose army are you fighting? Choose wisely because your choice determines which crown you will receive at the end!

Week 8

> Finally, be strong in the Lord and in his mighty power. (Ephesians 6:10 NIV)

What struggles or obstacles are you facing in your life today? Who or what is the source of your strength? Is it your knowledge, people in high places, or your success, money/wealth, etc.? Do you find yourself fighting hard and the results are not turning in your favor? Try relying on the Lord's power. Let the Lord Jesus be the strength in your pain and sorrow and watch Him deliver you. Nothing is too big or small for our God. He is mighty to save, and He will never fail you. Let Jesus be your anchor! When we take our eyes off Jesus and convince ourselves that we've got it, that is when we feel weak and defeated. Live in victory through His mighty power! Watch your strength grow against the enemy's schemes.

Week 9

> And my God will meet all your needs according to the riches of his glory in Christ Jesus. (Philippians 4:19 NIV)

Has God met your needs? Before you answer this question, ask yourself, "What is the definition of need?" The scripture did not say God will provide you with all you want. Yes, our God is a generous Father. He blesses us many times beyond our needs. After you define the word need or necessity, praise God for all the blessings He has bestowed upon your life, despite the different trials you might be facing.

Week 10

> And do not lead us into hard testing but keep us
> safe from the Evil One. (Matthew 6:13 TCJSB)

Throughout the Old Testament, God has always conveyed His heart for community or group, not individualism. If you study any part of Judaism, you will notice that Jesus's prayer covers the different elements that are common in their prayers. Jesus in His prayer reflects God's heart. God's plan has always been community, which He attempted to build with the Israelites. Some may wonder, why does Jesus pray for God not to lead us into temptation? Let's remember everything that takes place does not happen outside the will of God (Ephesians 1:11, Matthew 10:29, Psalm 24:1, Acts 4:27–29, etc.). God allows us free will, which started in the Garden of Eden when Adam and Eve chose to eat from the forbidden tree. Therefore, being led into temptation always manifests by our own desires (James 1:14–15). The choices we make using our free will can lead us into temptation according to our desire. Our free will either leads us toward God or away from God. What or who are you being led by to use your free will?

Week 11

> After that, he poured water into a basin and
> began to wash his Disciples' feet, drying them
> with the towel that was wrapped around him.
> (John 13:5 NIV)

Jesus was a servant. Jesus calls us to be servants not just to those we love but to the people in our lives who are unlovable (Luke 6:27–36). He did not just love with words but with actions in all that He did as He walked this earth. Can you imagine washing the feet of the person who you know is going to hand you over to a group of people to be murdered? I don't know what your enemies have done to you, but Jesus demonstrated that nobody is worth losing His place at the right hand of the Father. Jesus Himself says unless you forgive, your heavenly Father will not forgive you (Matthew 6:15). Who do you need to forgive from the heart today? Don't delay; the next minute is not promised!

Week 12

> Keeping a clear conscience, so that those who speak maliciously against your good behavior in Christ may be ashamed of their slander. (1 Peter 3:16 NIV)

How is your conscience? The context of the chapter is about the humility of our hearts as we tell the world about our faith and belief in Jesus Christ. Have you ever found yourself saying, "I don't care what others think about what I do and how I live my life"? As for me, I made that comment many times before I understood what it meant to no longer live for myself as a Christian. Since Jesus calls His followers to be the light of the world (Matthew 5:14), it does matter how the world perceives my behaviors. Can you confidently say your conscience is clear because your behaviors are according to God's standard? I don't know where you are in life. Assess your attitude and actions. Ask yourself, will Christ be able to defend you against your enemies while reflecting on your lifestyle?

Week 13

> But remember the LORD your God, for it is he who gives you the ability to produce wealth, and so confirms his covenant, which he swore to your ancestors, as it is today. (Deuteronomy 8:18)

When you have time, read the book of Deuteronomy. God's people were being reminded as they entered the promised land and became prosperous to remember it was God who gave it to them. Are we any different from the Israelites in our approach toward whatever you might consider wealth or blessings? How often do we boast about our success and forget that it is not our brilliance, academic achievements, people in power, or luck that blessed us with all that we have? It is God, Jireh (our provider), who provides us with all we have. Have you ever considered that everything you have can be taken from you instantly? Don't put your trust in earthly things. Put your trust and hope in the strength and power of God that produces all wealth/blessings, small or large (Deuteronomy 8:19).

Week 14

> But Peter and John replied, "Which is right in
> God's eyes: to listen to you, or to him? You be the
> judges! (Acts 4:19 NIV)

Read this Scripture slowly, stop, and ponder on Peter's question to the religious leaders who were attempting to intimidate him. Who or what is influencing your daily decisions? There are so many opinions and influencers. Who is the captain of your life journey? Jesus calls us to love Him above everything in our lives; otherwise, we cannot be His Disciples (Luke 14:25–27). Whose voices have you been listening to? Who is guiding or driving your daily decisions? You are the judge of that!

Week 15

> Does anyone want to live a life that is long and
> prosperous? Then keep your tongue from speak-
> ing evil and your lips from telling lies! (Psalm
> 34:12–13 NLT)

I recently read a statement that I can't recall the exact wording, but it conveyed something like: Lying has become the norm of society, therefore, telling the truth has become an extraordinary act. As you read these Scriptures, do you find your mind spinning like mine did? It appears to me that the opposite of what the Scripture says is happening all around us. It seems that those who lie and speak evil are winning, living a long life, and thriving in our society. It seems that virtues and integrity are no longer the standard in our society. Despite what my eyes are seeing, I know God's Word is truth. 2 Peter 3:9 reminds us that God's patience with the wicked is not slowness. In fact, God's desire is that no one perishes and hopes that everyone turns from their sins. Decide today to live a long and prosperous life with God's truth on your tongue! Let's not join the crowd that seems louder; let us be the minority who stands for godly truth!

Week 16

> For our struggle is not against flesh and blood,
> but against the rulers, against the authorities,
> against the powers of this dark world and against
> the spiritual forces of evil in the heavenly realms.
> (Ephesians 6:12 NIV)

What struggle are you fighting through today? Whatever it might be, the fight you are taking on is much bigger than you. Your mistakes, conflicts with others, addictions, sickness, being a victim of abuse, etc. are bigger than what your eyes can see. As you witness the chaos happening around you or in your personal life, know that the spirit of this dark world is the enemy. There is a dark force fighting for our soul. These spiritual powers manifest in unusual ways that often blind us from seeing beyond the physical world. For example, how do we explain the reason a person decides to take a weapon and kill others with no remorse? We can reason many ways why such an act takes place. However, when we hear or see these incidents that seem to occur so often in our society, we must train ourselves to see them in the spiritual realm. During any incidents, I have learned to observe how the spiritual forces of this dark world are using God's creation to dwell and carry out its evil destruction. God's armor is the only weapon that can help us fight against the schemes of the rulers and authorities of this dark world (Ephesians 6:10–18). Lord Jesus, please open our eyes to see the spiritual war waging against us all, so that we do not fall into Satan's trap of becoming hateful and bitter toward each other!

Week 17

> I have hidden your word in my heart that I might
> not sin against you. (Psalm 119:11 NIV)

When you woke up this morning, was God's Word the first in your mind? We live in a busy and stressful society where our heart and mind are always being tugged in different directions. Hiding God's Word in our heart takes persistence and intentionality. Jesus exemplifies the importance of hiding God's Word in our heart so that we can stand strong against the devil's schemes throughout our testing times in this world (Mark 1:35; Matthew 4:1–11). If we do not hide the Word of God in our heart, we are left with our sinful nature as the compass of our heart. As a result, our daily actions and decisions do not reflect the heart of God and lead us away from God's purpose for our lives and toward Satan's domain. I know personally for me, when God's Word is not hidden in my heart when I start my day, I can be less compassionate, short with people, and easily angered. Decide today that you will let the Word of God be the blood that pumps and regulates the function of your heart.

Week 18

> Rejoice always, pray continually, give thanks in
> all circumstances; for this is God's will for you
> in Christ Jesus. (1 Thessalonians 5:16–18 NIV)

Do you believe God's will for us is to put into practice each element listed in this passage? Do you speak to God through all your life circumstances? Or do you only pray during the drought periods in your life? Rejoicing always and giving thanks in all circumstances takes being purposeful and intentional through faith in God. It takes complete surrender and believing His promises are true. As I am writing this reflection, I have been struggling with sudden dizziness. My quality of life has shifted in one week. Staying in the Word of God, reading His promises, and knowing that as long as I am in this world and in this body, I will be attacked by the power of this dark world. We must decide daily that the spirit of this dark world will not guide our joyful and thankful heart, no matter what life throws at us. The day will come where all our trials and tears will be no more for those who remain under the wing of Jesus as our Shepherd (Psalm 23:1; John 15:1–8; Revelation 21:1–4). In your seasons of goodness and hardship, make a list of the victories, blessings, and trials that God has allowed in your life; watch your soul shout with gratitude and joy as you see the miracles in all of it.

Week 19

> The Son is the radiance of God's glory and the exact representation of his being, sustaining all things by his powerful word. After he had provided purification for sins, he sat down at the right hand of the Majesty in heaven. (Hebrews 1:3 NIV)

Do you want to know the intimate part of God? Spend time with Jesus, who is God's Word in the flesh (John 1:1–14). Is your life falling apart, where nothing seems to be working out? Allow Jesus, who is the sustaining force of all things and powerful words, to transform your life (Hebrews 4:12–13). Jesus is ready to change your life if you are ready to surrender your will to His purpose. You are never too broken or far from God to enter His presence. Jesus is waiting for you to come home, where you belong.

Week 20

> Taste and see that ADONAI is good; How blessed are those who take refuge in him! (Psalm 34:8 CJB)

Tasting can be a life-changing experience. Some tastes can lead you to a positive or negative life experience. What have you tasted in your life? How has it been going for you? The psalmist is inviting you to taste God as your choice of food or drinks. Oftentimes, you hear people say, "I became addicted after I tried —— once." You fill in the blank. Have you found that your choice of taste has become bitter in your life? The psalmist is inviting you to try God's goodness and confidently promises that tasting God is the best choice. God, through Jesus Christ, is calling you to taste His goodness despite all the bitterness that you might be enduring from the taste of this life. Decide today to taste the Lord and allow the flavor of the Lord to overpower any taste that has been burdensome in your life. God is offering to take your struggles and burdens from the taste of this life in exchange for rest (Matthew 11:28–30).

Week 21

> Iyov got up, tore his coat, shaved his head, fell down on the ground and worshipped; he said, "Naked I came from my mother's womb, and naked I will return there. *ADONAI* gave; *ADONAI* took; blessed be the name of *ADONAI*." (Job 1:20–21 CJB)

This verse is found in Job chapter one after God allowed Satan to strike everything that was meaningful to Job. The holiday is approaching. For some, it will evoke feelings of joy, excitement, happiness, and memorable times. And for others, the holiday will provoke feelings of pain, sadness, sorrow, guilt, shame, grief, anger, loneliness, etc. My prayer for each one of us, like Job, no matter what situation you find yourself in, is to praise God who can see you through positive and negative circumstances in your life. For we have a High Priest in Jesus Christ who can sympathize with us in every way (Hebrews 4:15).

Week 22

> When they saw the star, they were filled with joy! They entered the house and saw the child with his mother, Mary, and they bowed down and worshipped him. Then they opened their treasure chests and gave him gifts of gold, frankincense, and myrrh. (Matthew 2:10–11 NLT)

I love this time of the year! Not because I get to celebrate the birth of Jesus but because I get to share Jesus with the world. As a Christian, the celebration of Jesus's birth and resurrection (Easter) should be celebrated every day. In case you are not aware, there is no certainty that December 25 is the accurate birthdate of Jesus. Nonetheless, that should not stop us from using the opportunity to share the Good News of the Gospel with a world that so desperately needs a Lord and a Savior. Yes, the world uses Christmas as a time to indulge in materialistic things and oftentimes doesn't even focus on Jesus as the gift. Instead, many focus on themselves instead of the true meaning of Jesus who came to serve and not to be served (Mark 10:45). My prayer is for each of us to teach our children about worshiping Jesus, not Santa. Santa is a distraction that the enemy allowed the world to invent to stop us from teaching and focusing on God as our provider who gives us everything through the birth of Jesus, the ultimate gift. Let us bow down and worship our Lord Jesus just as the Magi did when they saw him. And let us give him the gift that He wants, a broken and contrite heart (Psalm 51:17).

> For to us a child is born... Mighty God, Everlasting Father, Prince of Peace. (Isaiah 9:6–7)

Week 23

> "Do not suppose that I have come to bring peace to the earth. I did not come to bring peace, but a sword. For I have come to turn" "a man against his father, a daughter against her mother, a daughter-in-law against her mother-in-law—a man's enemies will be the members of his own household." (Matthew 10:34–36 NIV)

There are many examples in our world that demonstrate Jesus's point in the passage above. Each of us can probably think of situations where members of our families and friends have shunned us for our faith in Jesus Christ. We live in a society that no longer appreciates absolute ideas or convictions. The words compromise, acceptance, and fluid ideas are embraced more as the norm. Jesus, knowing all things, warns us about the cost of following Him because there is no grey line or fluid ideas when it comes to God's commands and expectations (Matthew 16:24–26; Luke 14:26–27). For example, consider the word *marriage*. According to God, marriage is between a man and a woman. Jesus clearly reminded us in Mark 10:6–9 that God created male and female, and that is the union He approves. Apostle Paul in Romans 1:18–28 tells us about the mastermind behind the delusion of homosexual relationships and where their destination will be if they do not repent. In Leviticus 20:13, God's instruction was to put to death those who practice such a lifestyle. Hopefully, this example gives you a picture of what Jesus meant in the passage above. How is your conviction about the commands of God? Where in your life are you compromising the Word of God for the sake of society's definition of unity/peace?

Week 24

> Above all, you must live as citizens of heaven, conducting yourselves in a manner worthy of the Good News about Christ. Then, whether I

> come and see you again or only hear about you,
> I will know that you are standing together with
> one spirit and one purpose, fighting together for
> the faith, which is the Good News. (Philippians
> 1:27 NLT)

What citizenship are you defending and fighting for in your life? Apostle Paul in the scripture above was reminding the Disciples in Philippi about what is worth fighting for as soldiers in Christ's army. Do you know when you became a Christian, your citizenship is bound to heaven, not to this earth?

> If you belong to Christ, then you are Abraham's
> seed, and heirs according to the promise.
> (Galatians 3:29)

If Jesus is our Lord, we are all one unit under His authority, not the power of this world. Whether you consider yourself a Jew or a Gentile, Jesus came to break the barrier that separated us from God so that we are all one under God's sovereignty.

So then, why do we often let the affairs and politics of this world lead us to a road away from our heavenly citizenship with our Lord Jesus Christ? Why do we easily fall into Satan's trap to choose a side when there are always two sides to every story and the truth? Only God knows the truth because He knows the minds, hearts, and schemes of all men (Proverbs 14:10 and Romans 27:29). If you declare that Jesus Christ is your Lord, and you no longer live by the standard of your flesh, you are a transient in this world until we go to our destination. As Jesus said,

> We are not of this world just as he was not of this
> world. (John 17:16)

Presently, in this world, there are many nations at war. Our goal as citizens of heaven during these times is not to defend the cause of this world but the "Good News" of Jesus Christ. For instance, there is a season approaching that will expose many people's hearts and focus. The sad part is, during this season, many people who claim to be Christian will take the scriptures and use them to fight the causes of this world instead of what God calls us to do as His ambassadors. If you don't know what season I am referring to, it is called the election.

I pray that whether it's the election or any other world affairs, we will imitate Jesus by recognizing the matters of this world are not God's Good News. Let us not be deceived by those who come in the name of the Lord and who are wolves in sheep's clothing. Let us remember that no one is good but God. Just because the scripture is being used by someone does not mean it's to defend the nature or will of God. Go back to Jesus's encounter with Satan in Matthew 4:1–11. Satan's goal is to divide and destroy humanity, and God's goal is to save us from Satan's wrath and guide us to find the narrow road to our heavenly home.

Let us fight for what matters, bringing one soul at a time back to God. Let us not be so consumed by the sins of one group and become the judge and executor of men in a world that is not our place of citizenship. God is the only one who is the final judge who can decide the innocent or guilty (Hebrews 10:30–31). I am continuing to learn there is always more to every story than what my eyes see and my ears hear. Let's be alert and sober-minded (1 Peter 5:8) so that we can fight against the enemy's scheme to proclaim truth according to God's Good News!

Week 25

> Romans 12: 9–21 (NIV)
> Romans 12 reflection prayer

Father God, I come before You in the name of Jesus Christ, our Lord and Savior. I pray You will clothe us with Jesus as we wake up this morning and go about our day. Please open our eyes to see things through Your purpose. Lord Jesus, we are asking that You show us how to use our gifts to inspire others to walk toward Your throne of reconciliation. We pray that our thoughts will be continuously transformed to Your will, not ours. Give us discernment to test every thought and decision that comes our way so that we will speak Your Holy truth. Father, do not allow us to think of ourselves above anyone, create in us a sober heart in accordance with Your will and purpose for our lives. Grant us the gift of loving others beyond what we see. Father God, will us to hate evil and cling to what is good according to Your definition. Holy Father, do not take the zeal to serve You away from us. Please, Lord Jesus, teach us how to be joyful in hope and during difficult times. Help us to remain faithful in prayer, no matter what path we are on. Teach us how to be peacemakers and to live in harmony with everyone. Do not let us forget who we are in You so that we don't become conceited and look down on others. Do not allow us to retaliate against those who do us wrong. But instead, give us the gift of showing grace and mercy instead of revenge. Teach us how to care for our enemies just as You have cared for us, who were once Your enemies in our sinful desires. Father, teach us through the Holy Spirit how to overcome the evil that is all around us with Goodness, which only comes from You. It's in Jesus's name, our Lord and Savior, we pray and ask these requests. Amen!

Week 26

> Now the Spirit explicitly says that in later times
> some will depart from the faith, paying attention
> to deceitful spirits and the teachings of demons,
> through the hypocrisy of liars whose consciences
> are seared. (1 Timothy 4:1 CSB)

A friend and I were speaking about the subtlety of Satan's schemes in Christians' lives as we were contemplating all the things that even those who say Jesus is their Lord choose to compromise in. Every Christian should be on guard against Satan because he has been a deceiver from the beginning (Genesis 3—The Fall of Man), and he is still the same today. Apostle Paul's warning about Satan's scheme is alarming throughout his ministry. Those of us who profess that Jesus is our Lord and Savior are in a spiritual war. If we are not a student of Jesus through the Holy Spirit, we will be deceived by Satan's demons. You may say, "Not me!" If that is the attitude of your heart, he has already deceived you.

For us to be ready for battle, we must be aware of our enemy and acknowledge his strength. Satan knows the Bible and has been around God. We often forget that Satan was created by God; he has been in the presence of God and was a messenger for God before he rebelled against his Creator. A great study for every Christian is to learn who Satan was before his fall in the presence of the living God. How do you think Satan was able to tempt Jesus in Matthew chapter 4? He used the Word of God. Not once did Jesus deny that what Satan was saying to Him was not true. Nevertheless, Jesus was also a student of God and knew the full story to fight back against Satan's scheme.

Are you a student of the Holy Bible? Not just part of it or what might suit your belief but the entire Word of the living God. If you are not convinced the entire Bible is relevant to your journey with God, you are at risk of being deceived by demons like Adam and Eve in the Garden. Satan will use our zeal and devotion to God to make us agree with things that are contrary to God's Word. Look at how much fun Satan is having with our society on a basic principle of God's Creation. God created man and woman; marriage is between a man and a woman (Genesis 2:24; Matthew 19:4–6; Leviticus 20; etc.). Anything beyond that is from Satan and his demons (Romans 1:21–32). Apostle Paul warns us about these days that will come. He specifically warns us about Satan's scheme in 2 Corinthians 11:3,

> But I am afraid that just as Eve was deceived by
> the serpent's cunning, your minds may somehow
> be led astray from your sincere and pure devotion
> to Christ.

Let us be on guard against the enemy's scheme so that we do not forfeit the opportunity to see our Lord Jesus when He calls us home or returns to take us home!

Week 27

> Submitting yourselves one to another in the fear of God. Wives, submit yourselves unto your own husbands, as unto the Lord. For the husband is the head of the wife, even as Christ is the head of the church: and he is the savior of the body. Therefore, as the church is subject unto Christ, so let the wives be to their own husbands in everything. Husbands, love your wives, even as Christ also loved the church, and gave himself for it; That he might sanctify and cleanse it with the washing of water by the word, That he might present it to himself a glorious church, not having spot, or wrinkle, or any such thing; but that it should be holy and without blemish. (Ephesians 5:21–27)

Reading these Scriptures in the context of living under the authority of Jesus Christ makes so much sense to me. Oftentimes, I hear the first part of this passage being reinforced but not the second part. As a matter of fact, if we take the time to study this passage, I believe this is not applicable to all marriages. If a couple has not submitted to Christ, how can they show reverence or respect to His authority? Therefore, I believe Apostle Paul in 2 Corinthians 6:14–16 pleaded for those who profess Jesus is their Lord and Savior not to yoke with someone who does not have the same standard. It is evident by the Scripture that the instruction is to wives who are under the Lordship of Jesus as their Lord. Likewise, the instruction for husbands to love their wives as Christ loves the church is applicable to men who are walking under the lordship of Jesus. As we read the entire instruction, the apostle taught as if the people he is writing to already know about Christ and His church.

If you want a submissive wife, ask yourself: Is my wife under Jesus's authority? If you want your husband to treat you as Christ treated the church, have you married a man who is under Jesus's leadership? Yes, for this beautiful godly union to be created, both individuals must be under Jesus's lordship. Does that mean if one spouse is a Christian your marriage will not work? No! Apostle Paul gave us instructions on how we can win our non-Christian spouse over (1 Peter 3:1–7, 1 Corinthians 7:14). Even these Scriptures must be read in the context that you are living with a non-Christian and the knowledge that Jesus's commands are above all authority in our lives. Your spouse may ask you to do something that is not according to God's commands, and you must obey God instead of mankind. That is why Jesus says in Matthew 10:34–36,

> Do not suppose that I have come to bring peace to the earth. I did not come to bring peace, but a sword. For I have come to turn "a man against his father, a daughter against her mother, a daughter-in-law against her mother-in-law—a man's enemies will be the members of his own household."

God's standard for marriage is that it is built under His clear authority. Therefore, as we see many marriages that take place around us, we can easily differentiate the ones that are not under His authority. Sometimes a marriage starts under God's authority and, like many other things, we allow Satan to get in and change the course of the marriage, or a marriage that starts under Satan's authority and through repentance and reconciliation in Christ Jesus gets restored under God's authority. Let's examine our marriage and make every effort to stay or restore our marriage under Jesus's lordship. If you are single, heed the warning of Apostle Paul and decide which marriage you want when choosing a spouse.

Week 28

> I have come into the world as a light, so that no one who believes in me should stay in darkness. (John 12:46 NIV)

Growing up, like most children, I did not like the dark, particularly growing up in a Caribbean culture where you hear stories about what takes place during the nighttime. I also think of the many dark places that I have been emotionally in my life. None of these experiences were pleasant at the time. Can you relate to your dark places not being pleasant? Many of us don't even want to talk about our dark past because it brings so much pain. As much as we hate the dark places in our lives, for many of us, the scars and the emotional lifelong impact are not easy to escape. Many of us might learn, as expected by society, to put on a happy and strong face despite adversities. However, in the quiet moment when nobody is around, usually at night, it hits us like a bulldozer.

Jesus is inviting you and giving you an opportunity to no longer stay in the darkness. Our darkness is different and requires different degrees of light. The most incredible truth about Jesus's offer is that He can handle everything. No load is too light or heavy for our Lord. That is why only Jesus was able to take the entire world's sins onto His shoulders so that He could set us free from the darkness of this world (John 3:16–21). If you desire to be set free from the darkness of life, say yes to Jesus. No matter where you are in your life or have been, come just as you are. Allow Him to transform your life from the evil deeds that the enemy has against you to the eternal light of restoration and reconciliation with your Creator.

Week 29

> Do not be amazed at this, for a time is coming when all who are in their graves will hear his voice and come out—those who have done what is good will rise to live, and those who have done what is evil will rise to be condemned. (John 5:28–29 NIV)

The Gospel according to Jesus! I am always amazed by the teaching of Jesus. Do you sometimes find yourself attempting to wrestle with Jesus's teachings, where you try to reason or understand why God says, allows, or does certain things throughout the history of human creation? True confession: As I am on this path of reading the Bible and asking God to open my eyes and ears to see things through His eyes and hear things through His ears, I have found myself in more intense conversations with God. I have also learned from King David, even in my most distressful conversations with God, to humbly come back in humility, asking for forgiveness and reminding myself that God is God, and He does as He pleases. No man can understand the mind and ways of God (Romans 11:33–36).

During one of my moments of contention with God about Satan's role in this chaotic world and knowing that only God can stop him, I shared my thoughts with my husband, who cautioned me and brought me back to one of my favorite books in the Bible, Job chapter 40. During that same week, the Holy Spirit through Jesus led me to John 5:28–30, where Jesus summarized my perilous mind to one truth; there will be an end to all this chaos. When that time comes, we will either be on God's side and live with Him for eternity or on the enemy's side and be condemned. The questions we should all ask ourselves: What legacy are we building toward? What will we live for when we hear His voice on that day?

Week 30

> You see that a person is declared righteous because
> of actions and not because of faith alone. (James
> 2:24 CJB)

What does the word *faith* imply in your life? *Faith*, for me, is having complete confidence, loyalty, and trust in someone or something. What does it mean to you as you profess to be a believer in Jesus? As I continue to study the ministry of Jesus, I learn He had faith in God and therefore believed God's commands and promises to be true. Jesus surrendered His will to God's purpose and put His faith in God through obedience. To say we believe in Jesus and not have the faith to obey His teaching by allowing His Word to transform our lives is vain worship. James gave a perfect illustration in verse 26 of the same chapter,

> *As the body without the spirit is dead, so faith without deeds is dead.*

Yes, we can never earn our salvation through works, but the expression of gratitude and love toward God's grace and mercy is an expected response by God. In John 14:23, Jesus replied,

> *Anyone who loves me will obey my teaching. My Father will love them, and we will come to them and make our home with them.*

Our faith in Jesus Christ is the foundation of our expressed gratitude in action.

As you reflect on your faith in God, can you confidently attest that your daily actions have produced the deeds of your faith through your obedience to God's Words?

Week 31

> But godliness with contentment is a great gain.
> (1 Timothy 6:6)

As you read this verse, I invite you to join me in a moment of meditation. Godliness is defined by religion or religious groups according to their human understanding of the Word of God. As I study different characters in the Bible and see the different ways godliness is used throughout the entire Bible, it amazes me to see how a lack of contentment drives people to want more, which often leads them away from God. Studying Timothy chapter 6 is one of many examples of how this world's adversary (Satan) uses earthly wealth to manipulate us into believing that earthly gain equals power and that God is working in your life. I believe there are many people the devil has blinded to believe they are right with God because of their success.

At the beginning of the year, I was reading several posts by well-known Gospel singers and speakers; it dawned on me how most of the prayers for others and the world were focused on the manifestation of wealth and material blessings from God. The gospel of wealth and prosperity is one of Satan's deceiving spirits in the lives of many who are attempting to lead people to Christ. Having wealth and material things are not the concerns, but the teaching that wealth means God is working in someone's life is so opposite of the Gospel according to Jesus. Jesus warns us not to strive toward earthly wealth that decays but toward heavenly wealth that lasts forever (Matthew 6:19–21). Scriptures teach us every good gift is from God, including wealth. But when wealth status becomes the center of your heart and the root of your personal ministry in Christ, you are entering the enemy's domain.

Are you content with what God has bestowed in your life? Paul in 1 Timothy 6:7–9 summarized the Gospel according to Jesus very well for us,

> For we brought nothing into the world, and we can take nothing out of it. But if we have food and clothing, we will be content with that. Those who want to get rich fall into temptation and a trap and into many foolish and harmful desires that plunge people into ruin and destruction.

Week 32

> Be strong and very courageous. Be careful to obey all the law my servant Moses gave you; do not turn from it to the right or to the left, that you may be successful wherever you go. (Joshua 1:7)

When you are told to be strong, it is because you are going through a difficult time. I don't know what is going on in your life, but whatever it is, God is saying to be strong and courageous! Joshua was getting ready to lead God's people, who were not always easy to lead. As God was commanding Joshua, He made a point to repeatedly remind him to be strong and courageous. We all know when courage and strength are needed, fear is not absent. God provided Joshua and the people of Israel with the path to success as they were getting ready to inherit the promised land. The instruction from God was simple: obey Me, and you will be successful. No matter what your trials might be today, do not give in to the temptation of disobeying God's commands. The enemy has a way of making us believe that God's way is hard or takes too long when, in reality, the devil's ideas might seem easy or perhaps a faster route, but it always brings pain and heartache that are long-lasting.

> There is a way which seemeth right unto a man, but the end thereof are the ways of death. (Proverbs 14:12 KJV)

Week 33

> Therefore, do not let sin reign in your mortal body so that you obey its evil desires. Do not offer any part of yourself to sin as an instrument of wickedness, but rather offer yourselves to God as those who have been brought from death to life; and offer every part of yourself to him as an instrument of righteousness. For sin shall no longer be your master, because you are not under the law, but under grace. (Romans 6:12–14 NIV)

Do you ever find yourself using this statement: "Everyone sins"? You are correct! We are all sinners. If we were not sinners, then we would not need a Savior. Therefore, Jesus dying on the cross would be pointless. There are two groups of sinners. One group lives their life with no boundaries or regard for God's authority. Those individuals might have heard of God or even attend church as part of their routine, yet they don't know the Lord. The second group of sinners are those who recognize they have been given grace by God through Jesus Christ's sacrifice and, by the gratitude of their heart, they decide to no longer live for themselves. Hence, they have decided that their mind/thoughts and physical being belong to God. Apostle Paul's message in our weekly theme scripture is addressing the second group of sinners who have surrendered their lives under God's authority.

As I studied why Paul often reminds Christians that we are not under the law but under grace, I have learned we can easily become slaves to a set of rules. As a result, those rules become our God instead of worshipping the true God who sets the rules. On the contrary, being under the grace of God through Jesus Christ, our goal is not obligation to the laws or scriptures. Jesus, during His ministry, often challenged the religious leaders because they missed the heart of God.

> You study the Scriptures diligently because you think that in them you have eternal life. These are the very Scriptures that testify about me, yet you refuse to come to me to have life" (John 5:39–40)

Our theme scripture above is calling us to examine our lives. Then out of gratitude for what God has done for us through Jesus Christ, to no longer use our physical body as an instrument of wickedness. If you are not sure what Apostle Paul meant and how you can apply them to your life, begin with Galatians 5:16–26 as a starting point.

I know for me, the simple change I made in my life when I surrendered to Jesus was that I changed my wardrobe. I asked myself this: When I walked into the world, was the way I dressed conveying purity and transformation that I am an *instrument of righteousness*? You alone know who or what you are offering your body to. Is your daily decision an act of offering your body to God according to His standard, or is your body under Satan's authority? When people see you, do they see your body and mind as a reborn person in Jesus?

Week 34

> When hard pressed, I cried to the Lord; he brought me into a spacious place. The Lord is with me; I will not be afraid. What can mere mortals do to me? (Psalm 118:5–6 NIV)

Who and what do you turn to as you face hardship in your life? Every solution that is offered by our society is temporary. Oftentimes, most solutions that the world offers to our problems are conditional. God is the only solid and genuine solution to all our hardships without any condition. Whether we messed up or misused His solutions or blessings, He still loves us and seeks a relationship with us. When God is on your side, your situations have no power over you. If you have not done so, cry out to the Lord and watch Him deliver and set you up to win. Your spacious place will not just be on earth but in His eternal kingdom.

Week 35

> A person's wisdom yields patience; it is to one's glory to overlook an offense. (Proverbs 19:11 NIV)

Do you often find yourself offended by others' opinions, thoughts, and actions? For me, there was a time in my life when the answer would have been a resounding yes; I do get offended often by others. Through many mistakes and trials in my life, Jesus, through the Holy Spirit, has allowed me to grow in this area. There was a time in my life when pleasing people and having people like me was highly important for my self-esteem and self-worth. I struggled with this burden for many years in my spiritual journey. I said Jesus is my Lord/Shepherd, and I profess to believe that I lack nothing (Psalm 23:1), yet internally I was consumed by others' opinions, thoughts, and actions toward me. During those periods, although I said, "Jesus is my shepherd. I lack nothing," it was just a theory because the scripture had no influence and power in my life. How did I come to this conclusion?

One day, the Lord asked me why I do the things that I do. As I meditated on the question, I became emotional because I then realized my life was being governed by people and things around me. Jesus was not the Lord of everything in my life. I decided to work through the roots of Satan's scheme so that I could allow myself to live under the freedom of Jesus Christ. To experience the freedom in Jesus (Galatians 5:1), I had to face the root of my behavior, which was simply my upbringing. Growing up, I was ridiculed, verbally attacked, and mentally terrorized by people, and many of them were family members who were supposed to protect me. I never dealt with those incidents; the only way I harnessed my experiences was by striving to prove people from my past wrong and pleasing the new people in my life. Let me tell you, as Jesus freed me from those chains, I realized the burden I had been carrying for many years. It was exhausting.

When I am asked now why I do what I do, it's not for people or what my flesh desires, but it is to glorify God. Consequently, when people have their opinions and thoughts, and take actions toward me, I am no longer easily offended. Scriptures teach that these people are not my enemy. Satan is my enemy, and he will use any available vessel to enslave me and hurt God (Ephesians 6:10–13). I pray that God will allow Matthew 5:5 to be the precept that I live by:

> Blessed are the meek, for they will inherit the earth.

Meek is defined as quiet, gentle, submissive, etc. (*Oxford Dictionary*). As I continue to grow in this area, I have overcome bitterness, fits of rage, and hatred. I recall a simple practice that I implemented which has helped me grow in this area. I find myself making simple decisions like, if someone wants to be my friend, great! However, I will no longer work harder to build a friendship because at that point it's not friendship but a burden. In Galatians

1:10, Apostle Paul says our goal is to seek the approval of God, not men.

As you assess all that you do, evaluate why you do what you do. Do you find yourself hurt and disappointed by others often? What barriers in your life do you need to overcome to experience freedom in Jesus?

Week 36

> You will keep in perfect peace all who trust in you, all whose thoughts are fixed on you! Trust in the Lord always, for the Lord God is the eternal rock. (Isaiah 26:3–4 NLT)

As you read this Scripture, you might be experiencing a difficult trial where you are discouraged and feel defeated. You might find yourself asking, "Why am I not in perfect peace when I trust in God?" This passage makes me think of the story in Matthew 14:22–33, when Peter walked on water. The Scripture says Peter got down and walked on water, but when he lost his focus on Jesus and started focusing on the wind, that was when he started sinking. The question we need to ask ourselves during the difficult times in our lives is who or what our thoughts are fixed on. The Scripture says, "Trust in the Lord always, for the Lord God is the eternal rock." Learning to trust God and keeping our thoughts fixed on His promises during tough times is what brings us the perfect peace that God promises.

For example, knowing that on this earth we will have trials and tribulations (John 16:33) and knowing that it's not eternal because there is a time when our tears will be wiped from our eyes (Revelation 21:4). Those promises should bring us perfect peace as we trust in God through Jesus Christ. Our trials come and go, but God is eternal. Therefore, "fixing our eyes on Jesus, the pioneer and perfecter of faith. For the joy set before Him, He endured the cross, scorning its shame, and sat down at the right hand of the throne of God" (Hebrews 12:2) is the only path to the perfect peace we seek in God.

Week 37

> You say, "I am rich; I have acquired wealth and do not need a thing." But you do not realize that you are wretched, pitiful, poor, blind and naked. (Revelation 3:17 NIV)

Jesus wrote this stern rebuke to address the heart and mindset of the Laodicean church. This Scripture is very much applicable to our lives today. Jesus is reminding us that being rich in this world can easily lead us to worship our position in life and disregard the God who provides the "rich and affluent" life that we live. Are you in a position where you feel that you have reached the top and are in no need? Has your success become the focal point of your life? The Scripture above is a reminder that if our lives are not God-focused, we are doomed to eternal disappointment. If we rely on our earthly comfort to become our reassurance and protection, we are being deceived. The people in the Laodicean church certainly did not see themselves as wretched, pitiful, poor, blind, and naked because they were the rich and affluent people of their society. Yet, spiritually, according to Jesus, that is who they were. Jesus offered them true wealth and a new purpose for their lives. Jesus called them to embrace true riches and affluent lives, which is to rely on God.

As we reflect on the death and resurrection of Jesus during this Easter season, let's remember the wealth of salvation that Jesus has available for all of us through His sacrifice. If Jesus were to write about you today, what would He say about the condition of your heart? Do you feel desperate for God no matter where you are in life? Jesus in Matthew 6:19–21 conveyed the true treasure that we should all strive for. Let us strive to embrace the imperishable wealth that God, through Jesus Christ, has offered us, no matter where you might be in your life. Whether we have plenty or little, praise be the name of Jesus (Psalm 96)!

Week 38

> Likewise, the tongue is a small part of the body,
> but it makes great boasts. Consider what a great
> forest is set on fire by a small spark. The tongue
> also is a fire, a world of evil among the parts of
> the body. It corrupts the whole body, sets the
> whole course of one's life on fire, and is itself set
> on fire by hell. (James 3:5–6 NIV)

As I studied James chapter three, which I have read on numerous occasions, I felt a heavy burden. I started pondering how we use our tongue for many good purposes in our lives, yet if we are not careful, this important/special sense can lead us to eternal fire. How do we avoid using our tongue to produce *a world of evil?* Jesus, in Luke 6:43–45, tells us what we store inside of our heart will be the result of our speech. I have heard this statement as a young child that resonates with me: It takes seconds/minutes to make a mistake, but it takes a lifetime to fix it. The words that we speak matter. Our salvation depends on them. Let us think about how we can use our tongue wisely. That is why Scriptures say,

> For by your words you will be acquitted, and by
> your words you will be condemned. (Matthew
> 12:37)

Let's be more intentional about how we use our tongue.

Week 39

> For where you have envy and selfish ambition,
> there you find disorder and every evil practice.
> (James 3:16 NIV)

Envy (jealousy) (*Oxford Dictionary*): A feeling of discontented or resentful longing aroused by someone else's possessions, qualities, or luck. A desire to have a quality, possession, or other desirable attribute belonging to (someone else).

Selfish ambition (*Dictionary.com*): Devoted to or caring only for oneself; concerned primarily with one's own interests, benefits, welfare, etc., regardless of others.

Synonyms for *selfish* (*Miriam-Webster.com*): egocentric, narcissistic, egotistic, egomaniacal, solipsistic, egotistical, self-centered, etc.

How are things going in your life? Do you find yourself in disorder? Do you find that no matter how successful you are, there is always a longing for more? Or no matter what you do, the results are not what you hoped for? Take some time today to assess your heart and mind and see if there is any possibility that you are operating in the spirit of envy or selfish ambition. Maybe that's why your life might be in disorder and your decisions might be leading you toward evil practices instead of holy practices according to the words of God. Let's remember that ambition is different from selfish ambition. To have ambition to accomplish goals and dreams in your life is not a sin, but the motive that inspires or drives you to ambition can lead to selfish ambition. Allow God's compass to guide your heart and attitude and watch His power transform your life of disorder to serenity.

Week 40

> Jesus looked at them and said, "With man this is impossible, but not with God; all things are possible with God." (Mark 10:27 NIV)

Is there anything that is weighing you down where you feel there is no hope or no way out? I know we have heard this statement many times, "Bring it to Jesus," and it has become a cliché to our ears. When you are tempted to doubt God when life brings you situations that seem impossible and you are about to give up, think about the faithful men and women in the Bible who chose not to give up and brought their life circumstances to God. Let me share about a few of these heroes in the faith with you: Daniel in the lion's den deciding his God will save him and, even if He doesn't, he will still trust His sovereignty (Daniel 6); think of the woman who was bleeding for twelve years and spent everything she had, put her faith in action, and was healed (Luke 8:43–48); think of the Israelites as they saw Pharaoh's army coming toward them and they felt trapped because that is what their eyes saw, but God taught them He is a way maker even when it seems impossible (Exodus 14); think of Mary and Martha who thought the death of their brother was the end of the story, but Jesus showed them He is life; therefore, He can give life through the power the Father gave Him.

We can share several other examples of God displaying that He has no limits. When Jesus said nothing is impossible to God, He believed it, and He experienced it firsthand when He Himself was resurrected to life so that you and I no longer live a life that is restricted to what our eyes can see. Our God is "able to do immeasurably more than all we ask or imagine, according to His power that is at work within us" (Ephesians 3:20 NIV). Surrender to God whatever it is that seems unreachable, hopeless, discouraging, defeated, and watch Him use your situation for His glory, just as He said when He delivered the Israelites from Pharaoh's wrath. God, through Jesus Christ, has done many impossible miracles in my life, and I know He is ready to do the same for you if you let Him.

Week 41

> Therefore, since we have such a hope, we are very bold. We are not like Moses, who would put a veil over his face to prevent the Israelites from seeing the end of what was passing away. But their minds were made dull, for to this day the same veil remains when the old covenant is read. It has not been removed, because only in Christ is it taken away. Even to this day when Moses is read, a veil covers their hearts. Whenever anyone turns to the Lord, the veil is taken away. Now

the Lord is the Spirit, and where the Spirit of the
Lord is, there is freedom. (2 Corinthians 3:12–17
NIV)

We might read this passage and miss the incredible gift that
God, through Jesus Christ, has given us. What veil are we continuing
to hold over our face? If you have heard Jesus's call and responded by
confessing your sins, continuously repenting, getting baptized in His
name, and not living by the standard of your flesh, then you have
been set free! Therefore, you are no longer bound to the guilt that
we often carry as a veil over our lives. I know there are times I find
myself feeling stuck and confused. During those moments, as I cry
to Jesus for help, I usually find that I am carrying someone's burden
or my old sinful nature. Jesus says He is the way, the truth, and the
life (John 14:6) and He says those the Son sets free are free indeed
(John 8:36). Like the Israelites, we say Jesus is Lord, yet we continue
to deny His power by living under the old covenant. We let the opinions of the world around us dictate our mood and conviction from
embracing that we have been set free. Let us hold fast to the promises
of God as we strive toward holding on to the freedom that Christ has
gifted us, instead of living a defeated life. Do you believe God when
He says you are a new creation? Jesus took our burden, and tore the
veil that we had before we met Him. Let us live as free children from
Satan's bondage! That is why the passage above says, "Whenever anyone turns to the Lord, the veil is taken away."

Week 42

In the first year of Cyrus king of Persia, in order to
fulfill the word of the Lord spoken by Jeremiah,
the Lord moved the heart of Cyrus king of Persia
to make a proclamation throughout his realm
and also to put it in writing. (Ezra 1:1 NIV)

God's Words and promises are true and will always come to pass!
Have you found yourself doubting God in your life? I know that I

have done it so many times. In my season of doubt, I never doubt if He can do it, but will He do it for me? Or question why He is not doing it? There is so much that we can learn from the book of Ezra. Nonetheless, I was led by the Holy Spirit to read chapter 1 and verse 1, which resonated with my personal journey with Jesus Christ. In the past year, as I watched so much chaos happening in the world, I have found myself fighting to defuse Satan's lies in my mind about God's promises, sovereignty, and trusting His Words as truth. When the Israelites were allowed to be captured because of their disobedience toward God and were bound to slavery in Babylon, I can imagine the number of doubts and confusion they experienced. God, again, despite their outright disobedience, kept His Word as He had said through the prophet Jeremiah. The amazing part of the passage is the incredible demonstration of God's limitless and infinite power over the heart and mind of men. The Scripture says God "moved the heart of the King."

I have two questions for you: Has God been moving your heart to allow yourself to be used as an influence for His purpose? Are you going through something in your life that seems impossible, and you feel defeated? Our God, through Jesus, has proven, "Never will I leave you; never will I forsake you" (Hebrews 13:5). God has every right to shut His door in our face, but instead, He sent Jesus as the entry door to cleanse us from our sins and take us back from Satan's captivity. Jesus answered,

> I am the way and the truth and the life. No one comes to the Father except through me. (John 14:6)

Whatever you are going through in this life, trust our Lord because, in due time, your trouble will come to pass. Cry out to our God who can change the heart of men!

Week 43

> The eye is the lamp of the body. If your eyes are healthy, your whole body will be full of light. But

if your eyes are unhealthy, your whole body will
be full of darkness. If then the light within you
is darkness, how great is that darkness! (Matthew
6:22–23 NIV)

Dear heavenly Father, we come before You in the name of Jesus our Lord and Savior. We are asking You, Father God, to please help us see this world, which seems broken and in chaos, through Your eyes. Father, show us how to keep our eyes healthy so that our body will not stray away from Your light. Father, it is difficult to see goodness when we look around us and all we see is pain, injustice, greed, deceit, hatred, impurity, and so on. Our hearts bleed tears, and the earth groans (Romans 8:22–25) waiting for the revival of redemption. Father, we need a word from You as we desperately wait for miracles. Father, our eyes and heart say all is lost and there seems to be no hope. Father God, Your Words teach us You are the beginning and the end; You have the final say; You are full of compassion; You are the way maker; nothing is impossible; You are the miracle worker, and You detest evil. Father, hear our cry for mercy and justice. We feel powerless, but we know that we serve a God who is powerful beyond measure. Please, Father, in the name of Jesus Christ, do not let us drown as we look toward You for deliverance that can only come from You. Amen!

Week 44

Let us hold unswervingly to the hope we profess,
for he who promised is faithful. (Hebrews 10:23
NIV)

Have you found yourself working hard to remain focused on the promises of God? Let's be real! Saying that God is faithful and trusting God's faithfulness during trials are very different. Jesus understood how much faith it takes for us to hold on to God's promise when He addressed doubting Thomas.

> Then Jesus told him, "Because you have seen me,
> you have believed; blessed are those who have not
> seen and yet have believed." (John 20:29)

When we are tempted to lose hope and not hold on to God's promises, or when our faith is under attack, ponder the fact that you only see what is before you and we serve a God who sees the beginning and the end of your story,

> "I am the Alpha and the Omega," says the Lord
> God, "who is, and who was, and who is to come,
> the Almighty." (Revelation 1:8)

If we have been baptized and surrendered our life to God, our old self died. Therefore, we have been given the gift to have our lives hidden with Christ in God (Colossians 3:3). When we are tempted to doubt God's faithfulness, pray for Him to open our eyes to see beyond what the circumstances might be. I have been amazed at how much God has allowed me to see beyond my naked eyes each time that I have prayed this simple prayer that has calmed my anxious heart and reaffirmed my hope and faithfulness in my walk with God.

Week 45

> But you, LORD, are a shield around me, my glory,
> the One who lifts my head high.
>   I call out to the Lord, AND he answers me
> from his holy mountain. I lie down and sleep;
> I wake again, because the LORD sustains me.
> (Psalm 3:3–4 NIV)

As I read this scripture, I picture myself in the middle of a war zone that I must go through to make it to my destination. As I am traveling through that war zone, which seems never-ending, I am in protective armor that shields me from all weapons fired at me by the enemy. The war zone, for me, signifies the earth that we live in and how it is filled with different weapons of mass destruction. Nevertheless, we must navigate through and fight not to be destroyed as we strive to make it to heaven and to spend eternal life with God. The protective armor is the blood of Jesus and the Holy Spirit that protects us from the weapons the enemy utilizes and sets as traps to keep us away from our destination by destroying our soul. Are you protected? Who or what do you rely on for your security? Who do you rely on to give you high praise? Who do you call when you are in distress? When you call out to the Lord, what is your position in that interaction, a friend (John 14 and 15)? God says He grants sleep to those He loves (Psalm 127:2). How is your sleep going? Is God the sustainer of your soul when you are awake or sleeping? You know your life. Examine if you are secure under the protection of God. If you are not, start learning how you can be protected through Jesus Christ by letting His commands become your shield and your glory.

Week 46

> Everyone comes naked from their mother's
> womb, and as everyone comes, so they depart.
> They take nothing from their toil that they can
> carry in their hands. (Ecclesiastes 5:15 NIV)

Have you ever experienced moments in your life where you wonder why you do what you do? Many people have come before us and gone. For most people, after they die, their legacy and memories of this life dissipate over time. King Solomon, one of the wisest and richest men who lived in this world, had great wealth and power, yet he concluded that this was all meaningless. Since we are reminded by Solomon that we take nothing with us when our God-given Spirit leaves this body and dies, let us build a legacy in this world that we can potentially take with us, eternal life. Jesus says in John 14:2–3,

> My Father's house has many rooms; if that were
> not so, would I have told you that I am going
> there to prepare a place for you? And if I go and

> prepare a place for you, I will come back and take
> you to be with me that you also may be where I
> am.

Let us remember the wealth or possessions that we have in this world only satisfy the flesh on Earth, so let's strive toward the only gift that we can take with us when we leave this mortal body. In Revelation 3:21, Jesus gave us a glimpse of the only gift that is transferable to the next life after death:

> To the one who is victorious, I will give the right
> to sit with me on my throne, just as I was victori-
> ous and sat down with my Father on His throne.

Is your life a reflection that you are living a victorious life for Christ? Whether you have little or abundance, let us make every effort to harvest the gift of the Holy Spirit instead of the flesh (Romans 8:1–9).

Week 47

> But he replied, "The man who made me well
> said to me, 'Pick up your mat and walk.'" So they
> asked him, "Who is this fellow who told you to
> pick it up and walk?" (John 5:11–12 NIV)

As I listened to and read this Scripture at about 12:40 a.m., the Spirit prompted me to get up and write this devotion. I can, in many ways, relate to the man who was an invalid for thirty-eight years. I am very blessed that my deliverance in Jesus's name did not come after so many years. I was nine years old when Jesus brought me a Bible and called me out of the bondage of Satan. Moreover, I was fourteen years old when Jesus again delivered me from my invalid life.

Unlike the man from the story, people don't ask me, "Who is this fellow who told you to be set free?" Instead, due to a lack of belief and narrow-mindedness about the manifestation of the power of God in our society today, they either dismiss Jesus's powerful healing in my life or view it as fictional. God is the same today, tomorrow, and forever. His power and willingness to heal you are still available today. What is holding you in the invalid state where you are feeling defeated? Jesus is ready for you to pick up your mat and walk. Our invalid life may look different from this man's. It could be physical health, mental health, drug/alcohol addiction, sexual addiction, lying, wealth, etc. God is asking you, "Do you want to get well?" He accepts no excuses; simply get up and start your walk of faith and victory. Don't delay because tomorrow is not promised.

Week 48

> Fear the Lord, you his holy people, for those who fear him lack nothing. The lions may grow weak and hungry, but those who seek the Lord lack no good thing. (Psalm 34:9–10 NIV)

Have you ever reached a point in your life as a Christian where you feel weak and empty? This passage was given to me on a day when I needed the reminder that my weakness and hunger or feeling of emptiness is the result of my lack of fear of the Lord Jesus Christ. David was in a very vulnerable situation when this Psalm was written because he was facing what could have been his death. Yet he credited his victory not to his clever decision but to the fact that he feared the Lord. Who or what do you fear in your life? Could it be failures, success, yourself, rejection, or anything or people that you perceive as the authority over your life? The promise in the Psalm is if we choose to fear God above all things, we will lack nothing. This verse brought me to Jesus's encounter at the well where He exclaimed the water that He offers is *a spring of life*. Life can be very scary in this world, and we might even be tempted to conform according to our society. Let's remember to fear our Lord who promises us eternal life (John 14:6) and who "holds the keys of death and Hades" (Revelation 1:17–18).

Week 49

> It is not that we are competent in ourselves to count anything as having come from us; on the contrary, our competence is from God. He has even made us competent to be workers serving a New Covenant, the essence of which is not a written text but the Spirit. For the written text brings death, but the Spirit gives life. (2 Corinthians 3:5–6 CJB)

When was the last time you read and meditated on the Old Testament? Unless we understand what was before us, it is likely we will take the present for granted. In order to understand the depth of the Scripture above, I had to study what Paul meant by *written text or letter* in his writing. I learned the written text is referenced to Sha'ul, that is, written text engraved on stone tablets that were known to bring death because it proclaimed the guilt of the people. The writer is not saying the Old Testament/Torah is not important in our journey, but he is reminding us of the incredible gift through Jesus Christ. We no longer have to live under guilt because of the new covenant in Jesus Christ who has given us the Holy Spirit as our guide and counselor to lead us toward God (John 16:7–8; 12–15). This is a reminder that human competence or knowledge can't bring us life.

The Word of God is necessary in our journey; however, it is not the core of our salvation; the Holy Spirit of God is our bridge to our Creator. If you want proof that without the Holy Spirit and only relying on the written text or the Bible is not enough, look no further; look at the Israelites. They had stumbled repeatedly no matter how many times God gave them chances after chances to repent and obey His laws/written text. Or look at the Pharisees who studied the Word of God and taught it yet they were nowhere near God's truth (John 5:39–40). If you have chosen Jesus as your Lord and Savior, have you considered the power that lives in you?

I have a hard time understanding how so many preachers/teachers teach repentance, forgiveness, and salvation and yet minimize the power of the Holy Spirit by not reinforcing that without it, we are doomed for destruction in our walk with God. The Holy Spirit should be in every spiritual conversation and life decision that we make. Take some time to learn about the incredible gift of the Holy Spirit that lives in you. When we know and understand what we have, then we are better equipped to utilize and value the gift. Don't waste your treasure that will lead you to eternal life.

Week 50

> But remember the LORD your God, for it is he
> who gives you the ability to produce wealth, and
> so confirms his covenant, which he swore to your
> ancestors, as it is today. (Deuteronomy 8:18)

When you have time, read the book of Deuteronomy. God's people were being reminded, as they entered the promised land and became prosperous, to remember it was God who gave it to them. Are we any different from the Israelites in our approach toward whatever you might consider wealth or blessings? How often do we boast about our success and forget that it is not our brilliance, academic achievements, people in power, or luck that blessed us with all that we have? It is God, Jireh (our Provider), who provides us with all we have. Have you ever considered that everything you have can be taken from you instantly? Don't put your trust in earthly things. Put your trust and hope in the strength and power of God that produces all wealth/blessings, small or large (Deuteronomy 8:19).

Week 51

> For God does not change his mind about whom
> he chooses and blesses. As for you Gentiles, you
> disobeyed God in the past; but now you have
> received God's mercy because the Jews were dis-

> obedient. In the same way, because of the mercy
> that you have received, the Jews now disobey
> God, in order that they also may now receive
> God's mercy. (Romans 11:29–31 GNT)

I love the change of season! My favorite seasons are fall and spring. My thoughts during those seasons are always the same: My God is fun! As much as I enjoy it when seasons change, reading the scriptures above makes me so grateful that God's compassion and promises are not like the change of seasons. We often hear that the Israelites, who are of the Jewish religion, were God's chosen people, often referred to as Jews. Reading Romans chapter 11, the Holy Spirit led me to a truth that I do not recall ever hearing a message about: God's first selection to represent Him in this world. Think about the flood of Noah. Prior to the flood of Noah, God's intention was for all His creation to look to Him and find their way home. As you all know, instead, God in Genesis 6:5–6 (NLT),

> The LORD observed the extent of human wick-
> edness on the earth, and he saw that everything
> they thought or imagined was consistently and
> totally evil. So, the LORD was sorry he had ever
> made them and put them on the earth. It broke
> his heart.

God resolved that destroying mankind was His only option but saved Noah and his family, who were from His original creation.

The Gentiles—humankind—broke God's heart and failed Him, which led to His second plan. God decided, instead of working through the entire human race, He chose the nation of Israel to be His people with the hope of modeling what worshiping and honoring God above all things looks like to the world. They also failed God and broke His heart again.

God resolved to another decision; He realized only He can rescue us from the chains and trap that Satan has over humankind. He allowed His Words to become flesh, Jesus (John 1) and died for the whole world (John 3:16) while we were still in our sinful mess (Romans 5:6–8). Praise God that He does not change His mind about His love and promises to humanity. His goal is to save all His creations. When Jesus says in John 3:5–8, no one can enter the kingdom of God unless he is born of Spirit not the flesh, I believe God's goal is to bring us back to our spiritual form. God realized His attempts to work with us in the flesh has become a failure with both the entire humankind and Israel, as a chosen group.

That is why I believe Paul in Galatians 3:26–29 reminded us,

> So in Christ Jesus you are all children of God through faith, for all of you who were baptized into Christ have clothed yourselves with Christ. There is neither Jew nor Gentile, neither slave nor free, nor is there male and female, for you are all one in Christ Jesus. If you belong to Christ, then you are Abraham's seed, and heirs according to the promise.

To God, we are all under one redemption through Jesus Christ. To say you know God and deny Jesus, who is fully man—flesh—and God—divine (John 1:14), is to spread false Good News (Gospel). Jesus is the only door to God. John 10:7–9,

> Therefore Jesus said again, "Very truly I tell you, I am the gate for the sheep. All who have come before me are thieves and robbers, but the sheep have not listened to them. I am the gate; whoever enters through me will be saved. They will come in and go out and find pasture."

Let us rejoice and share the Good News that God, through Jesus Christ, is waiting to show everyone mercy, whoever answers His call!

Week 52

> In your struggle against sin, you have not yet resisted to the point of shedding your blood. And have you completely forgotten this word of encouragement that addresses you as a father addresses his son? It says, "My son, do not make light of the Lord's discipline, and do not lose heart when he rebukes you, because the Lord disciplines the one he loves, and he chastens everyone he accepts as his son." (Hebrews 12:4–6 NIV)

Have you ever cried out to God about a sin or struggle in your life that you want Him to take away? The more you cry, the more the silence grows. I have been there many times. God led me to this passage during one of my prayers regarding a trait in my character that I know is not pleasing to Him. Initially, when I read this passage, I did not understand what the Spirit of the living God was teaching me. I asked God to reveal to me what He wants me to learn from the passage beyond Jesus resisting Satan to the point that He willingly died for my sins. The one lesson God has taught me through this experience is that crying alone does not move God but a broken and repentant lifestyle moves God. As I read through Jesus's ministry, I see a pattern of speech every time He heals someone. He either reminds them to leave their sinful ways, not to return to their sinful life, or to go tell others what the Lord has done for them.

Our God is a merciful Father. He also has expectations for those who decide to follow Him (Matthew 16:24). God may forgive our sins, but the consequences of our sins are ours to bear. If the consequences were taken away, I believe God knows we would never learn and grow. One of the many examples in the Bible is *King David* in 2 Samuel 11–12. God forgave him of his sins, but the consequences were his to bear.

What sin(s) do you have in your life that you have not decided to drastically get rid of where your repentance feels as if you are shedding your blood? If you are pondering, how do I get to that point? Read Hebrews 4:12–13. God loves us and wants us to have victories. In our struggles, God might seem to be far away or neglecting us. He is only pruning us for His glory and for a greater path in our lives because we were all created for His glory (Romans 11:36). Therefore, through your struggles ask Him to teach you what you should learn because "He disciplines the one He loves."

ABOUT THE AUTHOR

A SINNER, WHO was adopted by the living God through the ultimate sacrifice of His Son, Jesus Christ, Annaika Dastine is a passionate daughter of the living God. Her gratitude for God's grace and mercy has led her to dedicate her life to being used as a vessel of God. Her desire, as God's Holy Spirit is leading her, is to inspire women to have an unfiltered view of the truth about Jesus according to the manifestation of His Word in their lives.

As she reflects on her journey with Jesus, she is in awe of God's infinite love, grace, and power. Through her past challenges and many trials, Jesus continues to lead her through the storms of life. She has been married to her best friend for over twenty years, and they have a young adult son. She continues to depend on the Holy Spirit and the mentors that God has blessed her with over the years for spiritual insight and guidance. Her desire is for every child of the living God to experience a personal touch from Jesus as a friend and Messiah.